ܠܘܛܒܘܬܗ ܡܪܝ ܫܡܥܘܢ܆ ܦܛܪܝܪܟܐ ܕܡܕܢܚܐ

HIS BEAUTITUDE MAR SHIMUN
PATRIARCH OF THE EAST

The Pitiful Plight of the Assyrian Christians in Persia and Kurdistan

Described from the Reports
of Eye–Witnesses

By

William Walker Rockwell, PH.D.
Member of the American Committee for
Armenian and Syrian Relief

WITH MAP AND ILLUSTRATIONS
Second Edition, With Statistics of Population
Edited by Nineb Lamassu (2008)

NEW YORK
AMERICAN COMMITTEE FOR ARMENIAN AND
SYRIAN RELIEF
1916

CONTENTS

FOREWORD

This book was first published as a pamphlet compiled from various archives, chiefly from the American Committee for Armenian and Syrian Relief, and includes not only eye-witness testimonies, but correspondence from one of the Assyrian patriarchs, Mar Benyamin Shimun, and his sister Surma D'Bet Mar Shimun. It has been clearly compiled with the objective of raising awareness of the plight of the Assyrians, to propagate the relief work of the aforementioned committee, and to reiterate the need for greater financial assistance from Western Christendom.

There is no doubt that this pamphlet, along with a few other publications, served to bring the plight of the Assyrians to the fore in the Christian West. They also helped shed light on the events of the Assyrian genocide whilst the dark shadow of Nazism was sweeping across the world. As a result of these publications, aid was made available and the lives of a people, reduced to deplorable and wretched conditions, were saved.

Today, just over ninety years from when the Assyrian genocide was planned and executed by the Committee for Unity and Progress (CUP) government, this pamphlet along with other similar publications serve an entirely different purpose.

The current government of Ankara, like all its predecessors, continues to take a denialist approach on *Seyfo*. The Assyrian genocide remains unrecognised in Turkey to this very day and continues to be a taboo subject that can not be spoken about. The biased curriculum taught in Turkey today propagates a make believe history claiming that the Christian minorities as subjects of the Ottoman Empire had, in fact, committed genocide against the Muslim majority. In light of such denials and an education system based on an utter lie, this pamphlet which is now being published as a book stands tall like a pillar of truth. For example, Rockwell, the author of this book, is clear about Turkish responsibility when he states, "During this period the Turks were responsible not only

1

for failure to protect the Christians effectively, but also for direct massacres under orders".

Having recognised the positive aspect of such works and publications, which are highly appreciated by the Assyrians, one must also highlight a pattern of flaws running through most of the Western scholars' perceptions and writings when writing about the Assyrians. As Dr. Roger Matthews the British archaeologist puts it, "books are written with the scholars' convictions and pre-conceptions". These convictions and pre-conceptions have often resulted in creating unnecessary confusion in the case of the Assyrians, which Yoab Benjamen – a prominent Assyrian scholar - clearly defines in a paragraph stating that, "a number of Western and western-oriented scholars who have recorded the history of the Assyrian people, ancient and modern, have in some instances attempted to deliberately mystify, shroud and even discard significant parts of this history. In other instances, they have ignored and twisted certain essential facts with regards to the ethno-linguistic identity of the Assyrian people. Properly speaking, these critical scholars have formed opinions and passed judgements that have no claim to validity."

For example, Rockwell's perception, like many of his contemporary Western scholars, is that the appellation of the term Assyrian is only associated with the Nestorians. Although he often and rather loosely includes the Chaldean Assyrians in this appellation, he completely ignores and excludes the Syriac Orthodox Assyrians (Jacobites), despite the fact that the latter probably suffered the most under this genocide.

In fact Rockwell claims that the Assyrians – Nestorians only according to his convictions – were termed Assyrian "for the lack of a better name". Rockwell also represents the first set of scholars that begun to mystify the geographical identity of the region. For example the title of the pamphlet refers to the Assyrians as the inhabitants of Persia and Kurdistan. However he often does refer to the region as Assyria rather than the new term "Kurdistan", which was just beginning to be coined. Thus when he refers to the first two missionaries that had visited the Assyrians he states, "The first two volunteers were the Rev. W. H. Browne, M.A., who died in Assyria in 1910, and Canon Maclean, M.A., now Bishop of Moray, Ross and Caithness."

It is exactly this approach which Dr. Roger Matthews criticises when he states: "the context of their interactions with the indigenous people of Iraq and adjacent lands may have been one of imperial exploitation, annexation and expropriation". This the Assyrians perceive, as Edward Said correctly describes, as if "an entire past was being kidnapped as part of building the orientalist discourse".

Nevertheless, despite these few limitations, the importance of this book should not in any way be underestimated. The reader should however be conscious of these issues when reading what is clearly a useful document for scholarly research.

Nineb Lamassu
Firodil Institute
2008

INTRODUCTION TO THE SECOND EDITION

The materials for the present pamphlet were drawn chiefly from the publications and from the unpublished correspondence of the American Committee for Armenian and Syrian Relief, of the Foreign Board of the Presbyterian Church in the United States of America, and of the Archbishop of Canterbury's Assyrian Mission. It presents also a letter from Mar Shimun, the Assyrian Patriarch, epistles from the Archbishop of Canterbury, and statistics of population before the war, arranged by regions.

Its preparation was planned at a conference called by the writer at Columbia University on the 16th of August, at which the following gentlemen appeared: Reverend W. A. Shedd, D.D., of the American Mission at Urumia, who sailed for his post the next day; Reverend R. M. Labaree, recently Chairman of the Relief Committee at Urumia and Salmas; Mr. Paul Shimmon, of Urumia, and eye-witness of the devastation of the preceding year, and the personal representative of the Assyrian Patriarch; and Dr. Abraham Yohannan, of Columbia University. To these gentlemen, to Mr George T. Scott, of the Presbyterian Board, and to Miss Rachel C. Schauffler, the compiler is indebted for suggestions and for criticisms.

To facilitate the study of the subject there have been included in the pamphlet a new map and a list of about twenty-five books and articles, chiefly in the English language. With the kind permission of Rev. F. N. Heazell, of Letchworth, England, the map was compiled from those used by the Archbishop's Mission. The table of principal dates is largely the work of Dr. Shedd.

The first or General Convention edition omitted statistics of population before the war, as for several reasons the pamphlet must not exceed seventy-two pages in length.

May this little publication be not merely a record of bravery in bearing the cross, but also a call to aid in the rescue of the decimated survivors of an ancient communion, which preserves in its liturgies a language closely akin to the Aramaic spoken by our Lord. Once pioneers in the penetration of Asia by Christianity, for centuries in their mountain fastness they have been loyal defenders of their faith.

WILLIAM WALKER ROCKWELL

Union Theological Seminary
New York City, November 1, 1916.

CHAPTER I

WHO AND WHERE ARE THE ASSYRIAN CHRISTIANS?

WHO ARE THEY?

During the past eighteen months a great deal has appeared in the papers about the sufferings of the Armenians and of the Syrians. Information about them from various excellent channels has poured into the offices of the American Committee for Armenian and Syrian Relief. The American public has learned that the Armenians are unfortunate subjects of the Sultan of Turkey; but nearly everyone is confused by the term "Syrian." People ordinarily think of the Syrians as living in modern Syria, that is, the regions near the Mediterranean that contain the cities of Antioch, Aleppo and Damascus. Actually men proud to call themselves Syrians are found not only in modern Syria, but also in localities as remote from the Mediterranean coast as are Mesopotamia, Kurdistan and North-western Persia. In fact, those Syrians to whom the American committee has thus far sent nearly all of the relief are not the inhabitants of the Lebanon's, needy as these may be, but the Nestorians and related natives of Kurdistan and North-western Persia, who for the lack of a better name are now designated Assyrian Christians.

The Assyrian Christians inhabit a portion of the territory known in Bible times as Assyria; therefore they are called Assyrian Christians. They also call themselves Syrians; for their Bible and other sacred books are in ancient Syriac and most of them speak modern Syriac.

WHY HAVE THEY BEEN CALLED NESTORIANS?

They have long been designated also as Nestorians, because they refused to acquiesce in the condemnation of Nestorius, Patriarch of Constantinople, in the year 431 A.D. The Differences between the Nestorians and the Orthodox party dominant at Constantinople were cleverly exploited by the fire-worshipping Sassanid kings of Persia, who tolerated the Nestorians just because they were not in communion with the hereditary enemy of Persia, Constantinople. In consequence of Greek persecution and Sassanid toleration, in the fifth century the intellectual centre of the Nestorians shifted from the Greek frontier city of Edessa (Oorfa) to Nisibin, which was then in Persian territory.

In the *Life* of his father, the late Archbishop of Canterbury, Arthur Christopher Benson writes: "As to their doctrinal position, though loosely called 'Nestorians' it is a moot point how far they are 'Nestorians' in the European sense of the word. My father more than once expressed his opinion that the heresy of Nestorius was to a great extent a question of language, and it is very uncertain whether the Assyrian Christians, or even Nestorius himself, ever professed what is now meant by 'Nestorianism'" (ii, 177). These statements, published in 1899, have been brilliantly confirmed by later discoveries of supposedly lost works of Nestorius, discussed in recent publications by Loofs, Bedjan, Nau, Bethune-Baker and Wigram. The ancient Nestorian question is now seen in a new light.

ENGLISH AND AMERICAN INTEREST IN THE ASSYRIAN CHRISTIANS

The missionary enthusiasm of the early nineteenth century rallied to the assistance of the Oriental Christians who were subjects of Mohammedan powers. The American Board of Commissioners for Foreign Missions early founded stations at Mosul, Mardin, Urumia (1835) and elsewhere. In spite of their initial determination to assist in the regeneration of the Oriental Churches from within, and to discourage the formation of specifically Protestant Churches, ecclesiastical differences between the American missionaries and the native hierarchies at length rendered that step inevitable. The surrender of the field to the American Presbyterians in 1870 did not alter this policy of friendly cooperation wherever it was welcome; and at the present time the Presbyterian missionaries have been, and still are, cooperating with the Archbishop of Canterbury, the Assyrian Patriarch, the Russian consuls, the Roman Catholic missionaries, and many other agencies, in the broadest kind of relief work; and several of them have died of diseases contracted at their posts in the endeavour to alleviate the misery of the refugees.

The Archbishops of Canterbury have long shown interest in the welfare of the Assyrian Christians. In 1842 Archbishop Howley, together with the Bishop of London, sent the Rev. George Percy Badger to assist the Assyrian patriarch in the education and improvement of his people. Dr Badger remained a year at the cost of the S.P.G. and of the S.P.C.K., but his support was withdrawn, so he returned. The chief fruits of his labours were the pioneer volumes entitled *The Nestorians and their Rituals* (1852), and a friendly feeling on the part of the Assyrian Church toward the Church of England, due particularly to the fact that Dr. Badger sheltered Mar Shimun in his house at Mosul during a great Kurdish massacre. In 1876, the Rev. E. L. Cutts was commissioned by the English Archbishops to visit Kurdistan and

The Matran Mar Khnanishu, Metropolitan Bishop of the Assyrian Christians (on the left) and the Rev. Y. M. Neesan

to report on what could be done to help the Assyrian Christians. At length, in 1886, the Archbishop's Assyrian Mission was put upon a permanent and satisfactory basis. The first two volunteers were the Rev. W. H. Browne, M.A., who died in Assyria in 1910, and Canon Maclean, M.A., now Bishop of Moray, Ross and Caithness. The Rev. Y. M. Neesan, in American orders, soon joined them. As it is evidenced in his biography, Archbishop Benson took the deepest interest in this attempt to bring aid, in the most catholic spirit of helpfulness, to this ancient Oriental communion. The Mission was maintained for a generation with headquarters first at Urumia, then in Van (about 1903-1910), and lately in Amadia. The commencement of hostilities between Turkey and the Entente Allies necessitated the abandonment of the Mission; but the circles in England who stood behind the Mission are now particularly active in the work of relief, as shown below by the letters from the present Archbishop of Canterbury.

HIGHLAND HOME OF PATRIARCH

During the early middle ages the Assyrian Christians were subject to the Patriarch of Seleucia-Ctesiphon, whose residence was a few miles down the Tigris from Baghdad; but the coming of the Turks as conquerors forced the Patriarchs finally to take refuge in Qudshanis (or Kochannes), a village in the highlands of Kurdistan. The present Assyrian Patriarch bears the official title Mar Shimun (My Lord Shimun.) It is said that he is the one hundred-thirty-eighth[1] Catholicos of the East, and the fourteenth who has resided Qudshanis.

---

[1] Editor's note: The author is clearly referring to Mar Benyamin Shimun. According to the most recent study of the chronology of the Patriarchs of the Church of the East he is the 104th patriarch rather than the 138th. Also, Mar Benyamin Shimun is the seventh patriarch that has resided in Qudshanis, and not the fourteenth. For a thorough understanding of this chronology please refer to: Benjamin, D, The Patriarchs of the Church of the East; Dinkha III not IV. And on the Patriarchs residing in Qudshanis see: Aboona, H, Assyrians After the Fall of Nineveh; Folded Pages from the History of the Chaldean

INHABIT A TRIANGLE

At the outbreak of the European War most of the Assyrian Christians lived in a territory triangular in shape and roughly one hundred and fifty miles on each of its three sides. One corner was at Mosul on the Tigris, just across from the ruins of Nineveh. From Mosul the Assyrian settlements stretched up the Tigris valley and also toward Lake Van, the largest body of water in North-western Persia. Then we complete the triangle by running a line from the lake of Urumia to Mosul, our starting point.

Within this triangle, geographic conditions vary widely. There are the torrid Mesopotamian plain at Mosul, the 4,600 foot plateau beside the Lake of Urumia, and the wild highlands of Kurdistan, 6,000 to 14,000 feet above sea level.

THE THREE MAIN GROUPS

The Assyrian Christians have been profoundly influenced by the kind of country they inhabit. We may distinguish three main groups. First, the inhabitants of the Tigris valley, from the plain of Mosul up the river into the hilly country, where the Tigris is known as the Bohtan-su. The total Christian population of this district is estimated at 80,000, exclusive of the Jacobites in the vilayet of Diarbekir. These figures include those "Chaldean" Christians who, as a result of persistent missionary work by the Dominicans and others have become Roman Catholic Uniats. They also cover the Protestants in Jezireh-ibn-Omar, about eighty-five miles in an air line northwest of Mosul, with its neighboring settlements, Monsoria (Mansuria), and Shakh.

Church, p. 96, and Haddad, B, Sepra Marduthanaya d'Alqosh, (Baghdad: Matdba'at al-Mashreq, 2001), p. 59.

A Kurdish Chieftain with two attendant Riflemen. Russian Soldiers in the Background

The second group of Assyrian Christians lives in about seventy villages on the plateaus of Urumia and Salmas in Persia, and in the mountains just east of the Turkish boundary. In Urumia and Salmas, as will be shown later on, the relief work has centered. The Christian mountaineers in Persia live in the border districts of Mergawar and Tergawar. The total Assyrian Christian population in Persia was estimated before the war at 35,000. This does not include the Armenians, who are scattered throughout some of the villages of the Urumia plain and are especially strong in Salmas. The Roman Catholic Mission at Urumia is in the hands of the Lazarists, a congregation founded by St. Vincent de Paul; and the Apostolic Delegate in Persia, Mgr. Sontag, played for some time a prominent part in affairs. Since the Russian penetration of this part of Persia (Adarbaijan) many Assyrian Christians have followed the example of the bishop of Superghan, who, in 1897-98 accepted Russian orthodoxy and control. During this proceeding the Anglican mission remained neutral, and later concentrated its activities on the Turkish side of the border. All these missions and Christian agencies have been co-operating during the present period of distress.

The third and main group of the Assyrian Christians lies midway between the preceding groups. It consists of the Highlanders, who live on the Turkish side of the border in Tkhuma, Tyari and other valleys near the headwaters of the river Zab. Just before the war their numbers were estimated at between 75,000 and 100,000. Most of them are members of the Ashiret or semi-independent tribes, who merely pay tribute to the Sultan. Their actual religious and civil head is the Assyrian patriarch, Mar Shimun, whose residence is in the mountain village of Qudshanis. Outside the Ashiret groups, there are a number of Assyrian Christians who recognize Mar Shimun as their religious head, but politically they are mere rayats (subjects).

In the closing pages of this pamphlet we present the most recent statistics, specially compiled for the purpose.

When Russia declared war on Turkey on the 3rd of November, 1914, the Assyrian Christians found they were living in a war zone. The three groups were variously affected.

Christian Womanhood in Persia

Graduates of the Girls' Industrial School at Urumia (since closed). The Rug in the Background is their Handiwork

CHAPTER II

EFFECTS OF THE WAR ON THE ASSYRIAN CHRISTIANS IN THE TIGRIS VALLEY

The first group, inhabiting the Tigris valley, was out of the line of military operations. We have heard from two sources that the Christians in the Mosul region were spared by the Turks, owing chiefly to the influence of their Roman Catholic patriarch and of the German consul at Mosul, Mr. Holstein. That some villages nevertheless suffered severely is shown below in the discussions of the death rate (pp.41-43). The Protestant communities, however, that were situated up the river in another vilayet, were massacred, as appears from the following extract from a letter of a Presbyterian missionary, the Rev. E. W. McDowell, of Salmas, Persia, dated March 6, 1916:

> "There was a general massacre in the Bohtan region, and our helpers, preachers, teachers and Biblewomen, with their families, fell as victims also of this massacre. The man who brought the word is known to me personally. This young man tells the story how by order of the government the Kurds and Turkish soldiers put the Christians of all those villages, including Jezireh, to the sword......
>
> "The three villages of Hassan, Shakh and Monsoria were Protestant and it is to be feared that they were wiped out, as were all the other Christian villages of the plain. Many of the women of Monsoria threw themselves into the river to avoid falling into the hands of the Kurds. Mar Yohannan and Mar Akha were still safe at the time-fled. The terrible feature about it was that after the first slaughter there were Kurds who tried to save some of the Christians alive, but the government would not permit it......

"This terrible calamity grieves me more than I can tell you. And more than those who died, the fate of those carried off into captivity weighs upon me."

CHAPTER III

HOW THE PLATEAU OF URMIA WAS HARROWED

The sufferings of the second or Urumia group began three weeks prior to the declaration of war, when from the 9th to the 12th of October, 1914, the Turks and their half-savage allies the Kurds attacked Urumia. A number of villages were destroyed and their surviving inhabitants fled to the city. The Russians protected the town and afterwards gave the Christians in the outlying villages weapons to defend themselves in case of attack until they could summon assistance from the city.

TURKS OCCUPY URUMIA

After the formal declaration of war the Turks invaded Transcaucasia, thus threatening the communications of the Russians in Persia with their base in the Caucasus. Therefore the Russians evacuated Urumia suddenly on the 2nd of January, 1915, Salmas on the 4th, and Tabriz on the 5th. Promptly on the 4th, Turkish troops occupied the city or Urumia, but from the 2nd to the 10th the Kurds and the Persian rabble vented their hatred on the outlying Christian villages. Owing to their overwhelming numbers very little resistance could be offered. Plunder, burning, massacre and rape were the order of the day. The terrors of such an attack may be readily pictured if we imagine a raid on defenceless Texas villages by a superior force of Villa's bandits, acting in harmony with the *de facto* government and goaded on by the Proclamation of a Holy War. Fanaticism was not, however, the dominant motive. On the 20th of May, 1915, the day that the Turks left Urumia for good, Mrs. J. P. Cochran, widow of the famous Presbyterian medical missionary, wrote the following vivid summary of the horrors and the heroism of the siege:

KURDISH DEPREDATIONS

"The Russians' departure was the herald for the Kurds to pounce upon the prey they had so long been held at bay from, and even before they arrived the Moslem neighbours in all the surrounding villages flew upon the spoil, killing Syrians, running off with their cattle and household goods and even stripping those who were trying to run away from them of their money, bundles and any clothes they cared for. They also carried off women and tried to force Christians to become Moslems, keeping them safely if they would deny their faith, or repeat the sentence which constituted the acceptance of Islam. In some cases they were successful in this, though, of course, many would not and some of them were killed for it.

"Then came the rush of the Kurds. They came in hundreds from every Kurdish quarter, sore against the Christians for having joined forces with the Russians who had armed them and drafted them for military service whether they would or not.

"They being armed put up a fight and killed a good many Kurds in the battles at some of the villages, though there were a couple of thousand Syrians killed, too, in the villages before they escaped to the slender protection offered by six unarmed American men in our mission compound.

SEEK SHELTER IN AMERICAN COMPOUND

"Our flag was put up on not only our property here in the city, but on all the adjoining block of Christian property in the city, and doors of holes in walls made between all that adjoining property to make it under our control and only our principal big street gate allowed to be opened, all others being barricaded. There in the city between ten and fifteen thousand, many thousand of them destitute, congregated and sat huddled in rooms, a hundred in a room or more, sometimes unable to lie down at night on account of the crowding.

"We had a good deal of money entrusted to us by the people who had to flee, and as most of it was in silver twenty cent pieces, there being no paper money in circulation here, they could carry away but little, and we took charge of large sums without interest, to be used by us if necessary and repaid when banking was resumed. With this we began to feed the people. It was the system in the city to sell bread until noon and after that to distribute one of the thin sheets of bread to each one who had nothing to eat and no money to buy any. This distribution took a force of about twenty or thirty men seven hours to get around with.

TYPHOID FELLS 700 GRAVES

"Then we all began to get the typhoid fever. We had some Turkish soldiers in the hospital with it and the people were ignorant and careless and we had an epidemic of it. We have 700 new-made graves in our compound here at the college as the result of it.

"In the city it was even worse. It is raging in our big compound, though from the first they had from ten to forty deaths a day from cold, privation, illness of one kind and another and perhaps shock from fright.

DR. PACKARD RESCUES 3,000 FROM THE KURDS

"In another part of the city, where we have a big school building for our Moslem boys' school, 3,000 people were rescued and brought in by Dr. Packard's valiant intervention, when he rode up to the Kurdish chief in the thick of a fight between

Kurds and the villagers in-trenched in Russian trenches and fighting for their lives. He begged the lives of the inhabitants, and after parleying awhile succeeded in buying the souls of the people in exchange for their guns, an rode back to the city with them after the sun had set on a January night, reaching the city about nine o'clock, their homes being robbed and burned behind them by the Kurds.

"Turkish rule and Kurdish plundering have reduced the inhabitants to the verge of starvation, and as yet the end is not in sight.

"There is no power of description that can overdraw the picture that is and has been before our eyes constantly of misery and distress. Instead, we have to veil it, for details are too horrible, too revolting to try to convey to people who are not called upon by God to go through it. But whatever the end may be for me, I am sure I can only be thankful God has given me such an unlimited opportunity for service as these past months have been."

Relief work at Urumia at once took on large proportions, as is shown by the following extract from a letter of the Rev. Hugo A. Muller, Treasurer of the mission, dated May 26, 1915:

"With the first inrush of people into our yards for safety came the necessity for providing bread. The first day it was done in an irregular way, each giving where he saw need, but soon bread was being brought in by the hammal (porter) loads, and we realized that it was an expenditure that we individuals could not bear. Mr. Allen took charge of the bread work for a few days until the village work required his attention, when Miss Lewis assumed the responsibility and organized the work in a business-like way, with a large and faithful corps of native assistants. This responsibility she carried until she came down with the fever, when it was turned over to me and I have been in charge of the purchasing ever since.

FIVE TONS OF BREAD A DAY

"More than 3,000 bread tickets, each for from one to three hundred persons, have been issued and reissued, and for perhaps more than three months a committee has been in constant session (under Miss Lewis's leadership until her illness, then under Mr. Allen until his illness, and since then under Mr. McDowell) revising and calling in or reissuing tickets. In spite of all this care the amount of bread distributed daily at one time rose more than five tons, but now it is somewhat less than that. We have been fortunate in that bread has been quite cheap throughout this trouble, but, nevertheless, by far the largest and most constant expenditure has been for bread."

The most notable detailed description of the siege of Urumia, thrilling but too long to give here, is in a pamphlet issued by the Presbyterian Board of Foreign Missions, entitled *The War Journal of a Missionary in Persia, edited by Mary Schauffler Platt,* since reprinted in full among Mr. Toynbee's documents.

The following narrative by the Rev. W. A. Shedd, D.D., of the American Presbyterian Mission at Urumia, covers the events related above by Mrs. Cochran and Mr. Muller. It gives a graphic picture and attaches responsibility for the massacres where it belongs:

THE FIRST FLIGHT FROM URUMIA AND SALMAS

"The retreat of the Russians put all Christians in peril. The Salmas Christians, except about eight hundred, most of the Christians of Tabriz, and eight or ten thousand from Urumia, fled with the retreating Russians. They left on the shortest notice, without preparation and in the heart of winter. Many perished by the way, mothers dying in childbirth, old men and women and little children falling by the wayside from exhaustion. This party of fugitives increased in number by several thousands from regions in Turkey between Khoi and Van, passed over the Russian border and scattered in the villages and towns of Transcaucasia. Many of them died of disease due to the privations and exposures of flight and life as refugees.

MASSACRE AND PLUNDER

"This flight left some 25,000 Christians in Urumia. All of these sought shelter from massacre. On the one hand the Kurds were pouring into the plain, urged on and followed by Turkish officers and troops; on the other hand, the Moslem villagers set to work robbing and looting, killing men and women and outraging the women. Several thousand found refuge with friendly Mohammedans. Great credit is due to no small numbers of Moslems, most of them humble villagers and some men of higher rank, who protected the imperilled Christians. In some cases safety was bought by professing Mohammedanism. Many died as martyrs to their faith. In several places the Christians defended themselves, but the massacring was not confined to these. Villages that deliberately gave up their arms and avoided any conflict suffered as much as those that fought.

SAFE UNDER THE AMERICAN FLAG

"The mass of the people fled to the city and all, including the city people, took refuge in the Mission compounds. The French Roman Catholic Mission sheltered about 3,000 and the compounds of the American Presbyterian Mission about 17,000. The latter were enlarged by joining neighbouring yards and so enclosing in one connected compound with but one gate for entrance and exit, some fifteen to twenty yards. The American flag was placed over the compounds of the American Mission and here people were safe from massacre.

"The villages in the meanwhile, with three or four exceptions, were the prey of plunder and destruction. Everything movable that possessed the least value was either carried away or destroyed.

GENERAL INSECURITY OF LIFE AND PROPERTY

"During the months of Turkish occupation there was never a time of real safety to Christians. The most unremitting efforts on the part of the missionaries secured comparative safety within the city walls and the people were scattered, to some extent, from the mission compound; and a few villages, including two that were not plundered at the first, were kept comparatively safe through the efforts of the Persian Governor. Beyond these narrow limits the Christians could not go. This was shown by constant robberies and murders when Christians ventured forth. During this period the Turks were responsible not only for failure to protect the Christians effectively, but also for direct massacres under orders.

GRISLY EVIDENCES OF WHOLESALE EXTERMINATIONS

"One hundred and seventy men thus massacred were buried by the American missionaries, their bodies lying in heaps where they had been shot down and stabbed. They had been tied together and led out to be murdered by Turkish agents. These atrocities took place on three different occasions; once men were seized by Turkish officers in the French Mission and sent out from the Turkish headquarters to be killed (among them being Mar Dinkha, the Nestorian Bishop). Once there were men seized in a village under the protection of Turkish soldiers and whose safety had been pledged repeatedly by the highest Turkish officials, and once there were men from just over the border in Turkey who had been forced to bring telegraph wire down to Urumia, and were then taken out and killed. In each of these cases some escaped and crawled out, wounded and bloody, from the heaps of dead and dying, to find refuge with the American missionaries. Beside these, the Armenian soldiers in the Turkish army previous to the arrival of Halil Bey were shot.

SUMMARY OF ATTROCITIES IN URUMIA DISTRICT, TO MAY, 1915

"In Urumia the total results in loss of this period, from the evacuation of the Russians on January 2nd until their return, on May 24th, were the murder of over one thousand people, men, women, and children, the outraging of hundreds of women and girls of every age – from eight or nine years to old age – the total robbing of about five-sixths of the Christian population, and the partial or total destruction of about the same proportion of their houses. Over two hundred girls and women were carried off into captivity, to be forced to accept Islam and to accept Mohammedan husbands. The Salmas district suffered quite as much as the Urumia, excepting that the mass of the people fled with the Russian troops, and consequently the crimes against women were not so numerous. About 800 who remained in Salmas, and most of whom were old people, with some of the poorer and younger women, were gathered together by Jevded Bey before his withdrawal from Salmas and were massacred. This happened early in March. The Salmas villages were left in much the same condition as those of Urumia."

No sooner had the Russians reoccupied Urumia, on the 24th of May, 1915, than the work began on a very large scale. It is described in the *Report of Relief Distribution in the Urumia Plain, June 1, 1915, to January 1, 1916* (printed in the Fourth Bulletin of the American Committee for Armenian and Syrian Relief, pp. 8-10). This gives the best account of that juncture in the distress and confusion of the Christians in the Urumia district.

REFUGEES RETURNEDTO THEIR VILLAGES

"At the beginning of June, 1915, when the people emerged from our premises emaciated from sickness and malnutrition and crushed by the blow that had fallen upon them, they were confronted by a seemingly hopeless situation. Practically all of their household furnishings and food supplies had been plundered; the same was true of their domestic animals on which they depended in large measure for their subsistence; their houses were without any doors and windows and probably a full third of them had been demolished. They were in terror about going back to their villages; they feared their Moslem neighbours who had despoiled them of their property, outraged their wives and daughters, and killed many of their relatives; they feared too lest the Russian troops might again withdraw and leave them to the mercy of their enemies; and they were anxious lest the missionaries who had sheltered them for the previous months, might forget them when they were out of sight. Everything tended to make them cling to our Mission compounds or their vicinity. To permit them to do this was of course out of the question. Our efforts, however, to scatter them to their village homes formed one of the pitiful phases of our relief work. The people had to go; but as long as they received their bread form our yards they would not; and so we had no choice but to cut off the food supply, after

> giving each family sufficient flour to support them a week."

As always, so now, the Relief Committee endeavoured to bring the refugees to self-support. They were sent by degrees back to the land, so that for a period of three months virtually all food distribution ceased. During this stage of the work the Committee distributed to the plundered peasants no less than 2,661 sickles and scythes, and 1,129 spades.

By the beginning of August prospects were growing brighter; but then a Turkish drive in another portion of the war zone forced the Russians to evacuate Urumia for the second time.

THE SECOND EXODUS FROM URMIA

> "With the going of their protectors the whole Christian population of the plain, with the exception of some 200 sick and aged who again took refuge in the Mission yards, fled, some only to the northern edge of the plain, but many to Salmas and Khoi and even Julfa. Fortunately it was summer time; but even so the misery was intense, and cholera and want and hardship claimed many victims in those few weeks. Worse still, much that the people had reclaimed of their stolen property and gathered from the fields was taken once more by their Moslem neighbors; and so after nearly a month of miserable hardship and uncertainty, the poor Syrians and Armenians returned to their twice plundered homes. Very little relief, however, was given during the next few weeks; for from the fields and vineyards much still could be secured in the way of food.

> "At this time we calculated that about 10,000 to 15,000 of the Christian inhabitants would have to be supported during the winter months, and we were making our plans accordingly, when a new and overwhelming burden descended upon us."

The burden was the arrival of about 30,000 Assyrian Highlanders, who, as we shall read in a later portion of this pamphlet, had fled to Persia for their lives. Relief work was prompt for them in the district of Salmas, but thousands soon began to pour over the pass from Salmas into the plain of Urumia. The ruined villages of the Urumia district, already crowded, had to give shelter to nearly 16,000 refugees from other regions. Fortunately the price of wheat was then very low, as the farmers wanted to turn their crops into cash and buyers were few; so great stores of wheat were readily secured. Then accurate lists of the refugees were compiled, to serve as a basis of distribution.

The problem of bedding was also pressing. Urumia lies 4,600 feet above sea level and is cold in winter. The fugitives had fled in summer with what they could carry on their backs, and had little to keep them warm. The lack of means of transportation made it necessary to use local supplies of wool and cotton, and the quickest and most effective thing to do was to make quilts. Therefore the missionaries started a quilt factory, which turned out woollen quilts big enough to cover several persons. Only one could be issued to a family, so that some of the large families of the Highlanders had to sleep in relays, and shiver the rest of the time. "But in spite of their inadequacy, the 5,510 quilts issued have saved the lives of many, for literally thousands were facing the rigors of winter without any bedding whatsoever."

The number of those in the plain of Urumia alone who received aid in November and December, 1915, was 29,512. In their support the Russian government co-operated, as did the Archbishop of Canterbury and other friends of the Oriental Christians; but it was a frightful period, especially for the little children. In January, 1916, a missionary wrote from Urumia as follows:

"Today is a wet, shivery, snowy day, the first wintry day we've had, and in every one of the score or more of villages round about us are thousands of shivering, naked children huddled close together in dark, airless cellars, in stables, in partly enclosed balcony-like places, grateful for a scrap of dry bread. Hundreds are still lying sick with this same dry bread as their only nourishment and these miserable holes as their only homes; until we who have seen so much of it all through this awful year have almost ceased to fell even a pang at the sight of the long rows of graves in the village cemeteries. Personally, I feel it a cause of thanksgiving that there are several thousands less of children than there were last New Year to suffer the miseries of hunger, cold, sickness and exile."

Though in 1915 the Presbyterian Mission in Urumia distributed $105,000 in relief, aside from war levies, ransoms, etc, conditions were still frightful.

Refugee Children on Christmas Day, 1915, wearing clothing just given to them by the Madame Nikitine, wife of the Russian Consul at Urumia

The year of our Lord 1916 began with such an overdraft on the resources of the Relief Committee in Urumia that it had for a while to close down all its work of distribution. Then the Russian Consul, Mr. Nikitine, whose efforts on behalf of the sufferers are most highly regarded by all acquainted with the facts, received funds from the Relief Committee of the Caucasus, and distributed them through the various missions in Urumia. For this official the Presbyterian Mission distributed 35,500 rubles in cash and over 7,000 garments and quilts.

Then with true foresight the Relief Committee began to buy up all kinds of seed; including wheat, barley, rice, millet, potatoes, beans, etc,; and many of these varieties it had to import by wagon or caravan from long distances. For ploughing it was possible to secure only 261 buffaloes and oxen. These were not given away, but held in such a way as to secure maximum usefulness. Similarly the amount of seed allotted was to be returned, with 50 per cent more to pay the wages of the overseers.

Later in the spring the funds sent to the Russian Consul were restricted to the relief of the refugees from Turkey (chiefly the Assyrian Highlanders), so that the Relief Committed had to issue some wheat to needy inhabitants of the Urumia plain. It was also necessary for a time to feed over a thousand Kurdish or Sunni (Moslem) fugitives.

In closing the Report of Relief Work in the Plain of Urumia, January 1 to April 30, 1916, the Rev. R. M. Labaree makes the following recommendations born of bitter experience:

> "A large number of spades and sickles will undoubtedly be needed by the very poor to help them to get work for themselves in the vineyards and harvest fields. If any bedding or clothing is to be provided for the coming winter, it should be

prepared this summer and not wait until cold weather is upon us as last year. Undoubtedly there will be intense poverty next fall and winter with high prices for all foodstuffs. It is a situation that causes us great concern."

DISMAL PROSPECTS FOR NEXT WINTER

The latest comprehensive picture of the situation in Urumia is given in the following letter from H. P. Packard, M.D., dated July 21, 1916. It is addressed to Mr. Paul Shimmon, who communicated it to the *New York Times* of September 18th. The explanatory notes, in square brackets, have been revised by the complier of this pamphlet.

"Relief burdens are still very heavy, and it is hard to know what is the least that we can do for the sake of the Christians. You know from personal experience how hard it is to get the Moslem masters [who as a rule own the land on which Christians live] to do anything for their Christian subjects. We do not want to use relief money for the advantage of these masters, but it may be that in many cases Christians cannot get any help from their masters to re-roof their homes, and may have to sit in ruins if we do not do something for them. [The village masters, as a rule, have also been hard-hit by the war.] It may be that by giving them part of the timber we may be able to induce master to supply the remainder. We sincerely hope that there will not have to be as much crowding during the coming winter as there was in the past. [It is the third winter in Urumia and Salmas since they were destroyed.] Some of the villages, such as Balou, Gachen, Walinda, and Geogtapa have been terribly crowded with the people of Tergawar, Dasht, and Mergawar [districts on the Perso-Turkish border which had been harried even before the war began], besides many from Marbishoo and Nochea [Turkish frontier], as well as some from Tyari and other places in the mountains over the border. The Matran [Metropolitan Bishop of the Nestorian Church living in Nochea, Turkey, near the border] has gone to Umbi, in Tergawar, and is now sitting there, and others are beginning to push up toward the foothills; but I fear that there will be no earnest effort to get these people established for the winter, and we may expect them to return to the plain, even if peace should be declared in the fall. [This was written before August, when the Turks recaptured Bitlis and Moush, towns which have since come once more into Russian hands.] Their villages are entirely in ruins, and there is no timber to be found without taking it from the Urumia plain, and the scarcity of cattle will make it impossible to accomplish this work this autumn, even if it were considered safe for the people to go back now, and we cannot get this assurance from the authorities. Some movement has begun toward Bashkala [on the Turkish border], but it promises to be small, and the investigation made in the mountains by David, the brother of Mar Shimun, and Malick Khoshaba and Malick Ismael, and their men makes them feel that there is no hope of getting back to their homes before the winter. This means that the mountaineers [the bulk of the Nestorian Christians] will be on us for another winter, and that relief work in Urumia will be heavy for some time. These mountaineers have had no fields to sow; they have no harvest. They have had to depend on charity so far, and will have to depend on relief until they can return to their homes.

OUTLOOK FOR FOOD AND CLOTHING

"We already have begun to make quilts. We shall make 2,000 now and 2,000 or 3,000 in the fall if we see that there is need for them. We have also arranged to spend $3,000 for simple garments to be ready for the late fall. I succeeded in concluding the first wheat purchase today. We got fifty loads at 65 krans (about $8 now), and have had 200 loads offered in dole for 60 krans per load. The crops are small here, and we expect that prices will be high this year, for there was no sowing in Tergawar, Dasht, or Mergawar, and the Sulduz sowing was much less than usual, and much of the young wheat has been pastured. The Anzal crop is about half of the normal, and Somai also cannot furnish much for outside. [These are fertile districts in non-combatant Persia, but crushed by war conditions.]

WHAT IS OUR CHRISTIAN DUTY TO THE KURDS?

"One of the greatest needs of the present time is that among the Kurds. I realise that this question will not be popular with many Christians in America, as well as in Persia. The Begzadi Kurds who are left on this side of the border are rayats (subjects) and not servants of the chiefs, who are the riflemen. We all know that when fortune favours them these rayats are almost as predatory as the servant class, but when the servants ran off with the chiefs they stripped the rayats of everything that they could take away, and we see these people starving now. They have nothing to reap for the coming year, so their condition is far more deplorable than that of the Christians. There will be few to appeal for the Kurds, but this is an opportunity that Christendom is not likely to have again. If we would follow the teachings of the Christ whom we profess to follow we would pray more for these same Kurds than we have, and we should be glad in this time of their great need to give them and show them that the Master's teaching is different than that of their prophet."

We may summarize the plight of the Nestorian and other racially related Christian groups native to the Plain of Urumia, Province of Adarbaijan, as follows:

They have been raided by the Turks, and by the Kurds, relieved by the Russians, then conquered and occupied for over four months by the Turks, relieved a second time by the Russians, who still hold the country, in spite of the panicky flight of August, 1915. They have suffered the horrors of a war zone, and have been inundated with refugees even more wretched than themselves. They have had epidemics of typhoid, dysentery and other diseases, and have had to survive on rations of coarse bread and salt. In spite of their losses they have the will to live and are headed toward self-support. The sufferings of this, the second of the three great groups, are bitter enough; but after all the place of honor belongs to the third division, the mountaineers of Mar Shimun.

CHAPTER IV

MAR SHIMUN'S HIGHLANDERS AND THEIR FIGHT FOR LIFE, AS DEPICTED IN THE THRILLING NARRATIVE OF MR. SHLEMON, OF BERWAR

The third group of the Assyrian Christians are the mountaineers in the valleys of the Great Zab. Their troubles began very promptly, months before the Armenian massacres.

KURDS TAKE COUNSEL TOGETHER AGAINST CHRISTIANS

Mr. Abraham Shlemon, of Berwar, long connected with the American Mission, an exceptionally well-informed eye witness of the defence of the Christians, has stated[2] that in the fall of 1914, when the Turks began to take part in the war against Russia and her allies, all the sheikhs, aghas, and various heads of all kinds of Kurds from Neri and Rowanduz on the east, and south to Jezireh north of Mosul, including all the tribes in the regions of the Tigris and of the Great Zab, were planning and making great preparations for the spring of 1915, to combine and sweep over the lands of the Christians and to exterminate them all. They had often said that these are "the little Russia"; if we kill these, then "the big Russia" will be powerless in these regions.

JEALOUSY OF RUSSIAN INFLUENCE

It is a fact that Russian influence had been steadily extending in Persia. In consequence of the Anglo-Russian Convention of 1907 the province of Azerbaijan (Adarbaijan) had passed actually under Russian influence. Russian troops had occupied its capital Tabriz on April 30, 1909 and the city of Urumia in December, 1911. Add to this the fact that the entire Assyrian diocese of Superghan,

---

[2] Mr. Shlemon wrote out his experiences in Syriac for Mr. Shimmon, who translated the remarkable narrative and then revised the translation in conference with the compiler of this pamphlet.

Persia, had gone over to the Russian Church in 1897-1898, and we see why the Turks might well fear lest the Assyrian Highlanders of Turkey would sympathize with the great Christian power of Russia.

BROTHER OF PATRIARCH ARRESTED

Therefore, in the spring of 1915 the Turkish authorities arrested Hormuzd, a brother of Mar Shimun, then a student in Constantinople, and took him to Mosul, to be held as a hostage until Mar Shimun should enter the war against Russia. What has become of the Patriarch's brother is not known to this day. Mar Shimun himself took refuge in Diz, in the mountains, some four hours from Qudshanis.

MAR SHIMUN APPEALS TO GERMAN CONSUL

"In the latter part of March, 1915, when the storm was about to break against all the tribes of Christians, Mar Shimun made an effort to avert the calamity by appealing to the German consul at Mosul. As we learn from Mr. Shlemon, Mar Shimun asked one of his chieftains farther in the interior to forward a letter to that official, Mr. Holstein, begging him not to listen to the stories circulated by the Kurds, who were intent on the wholesale murder of the Christians, and to do whatever was in his power to defend them. When this letter was carried to the German Consul, be it said to his credit that he was able for a time to stay the attacks, and he secured the issue of firmans in Turkish language that if any Christians were murdered they would hang every Kurd implicated. The immediate result was that for a time the Kurds were kept quiet and the danger was temporarily averted.

Kurdish and Christian Frontiersmen from Tergawar and Dasht

SAVAGARY OF THE RETREATING TURKS

"Meanwhile, however, Halil Bey [a relative of Enver Pasha], who was at the head of the Turkish army operating against Russia in north-western Persia, met a crushing defeat in the plain of Salmas on the 2nd of May, 1915. When retiring in despondency his army massacred all the villagers of Gawar on their way west, so that the Nestorian villages of Gagoran, Pirzalan, Maskhudawa, Mamikan, Diza and Zezan were destroyed. They killed nearly one thousand people, carried a great number captive, and took all their cattle. Some families lost as many as seventy head of cattle a piece. But as the Russians advanced later on, the Kurdish tribes and Turks of those regions, including those of Bashkala, Van, Moush and Bitlis left and fled, killing everything that came along in their route and devastating the whole region. Very soon after this, widespread rumours were circulated that the Christians would be massacred.

THE VALI OF MOSUL ATTACKS THE MOUNTAINEERS

"In the early part of June the Vali of Mosul began to get ready and collect a big army against the Nestorians. He had some 7,000 Turkish troops with regular artillery and some 15,000 Kurds from all those regions. In twelve days they reached Berwar and Amadia, on the banks of the Great Zab, a tributary of the Tigris. A few days before this some fourteen villages out of twenty-one in Berwar had made their escape towards Tyari, on the other side of the River Zab. It was then hoped that the Russian army would penetrate these wild mountainous regions and hold them for good. On June 18th (N.S.) the Vali of Mosul, Rashid Pasha, reached Berwar and after a few days' rest attacked Tyari, from Asheta the largest village to Lezan of Malick Khoshaba. Then when the people of Lower Tyari, the refugees from Berwar and the other Syrians saw that the strength of the Turks was greater than they could alone combat, they crossed the River Zab and destroyed the Khiu bridge and also the bridge of Malick Ismael de Chamba, which is a little north; and they also destroyed the bridge on the Lower Tyari below Julamerk.

AN ARMED EXODUS TOWARD THE RUSSIAN LINES

"A few days later the sister of the Patriarch wrote to her brother, who had in the meanwhile come to the Russian commanding officer at Salmas in Persia to ask for assistance, saying that the Lower Tyari had already been destroyed by the Turkish army. All that Mar Shimun could get in the way of assistance was some 200 rifles of an old type and a few rounds of ammunition and a few hundred Cossacks. The latter were given to him as escort for a certain distance to act as a rearguard. They returned again, and the Patriarch with his own men were left alone to venture into the interior of the country. On the way near Qudshanis they met bands of Kurds hiding behind the rocks north of Diz, and when they saw them, on June 28th (N.S.), after a sharp skirmish they fled. On reaching Qudshanis, Mar Shimun delivered an address to his men, asking them to defend their lives and honour of their families and freedom against their persecutors.

REFUGEES BATTLE FOR THEIR LIVES

"The battle in the meanwhile was going on between the Vali and the Assyrian Highlanders. The majority of the villages were, however, empty and the inhabitants were terror stricken and fleeing; everything was deserted. They had gone to the top of the mountains with their families, men staying behind to offer resistance to the big armies confronting them. The mountains are so steep here in Waltu that when the Christians saw some dead bodies in the deep valleys they could not climb down to them, but tied on ropes, thus descended to the valleys, where they found they were bodies of some Kurds. They took off their precious weapons and ascended with ropes again. For a time here the Kurds got the worst of it, and a great number fell before Christian tribes. The latter were fighting on the east and the Vali on the west, with the River Zab between them. But the Christians could not accomplish much against superior modern artillery which was brought against these regions for the first time in their history, and the people were terror stricken. The villages of Sarispedo and Asheta, the latter a place of 500 families, were destroyed, as were also Geramon, Arosh, Halmon, Zaweta, Minyanish, Margi, Leza and Zarni, with ten villages of Berwar. They destroyed over fifteen churches and took off all their old manuscripts and service books, kept for generations. It seems again evident that Mr. Holstein, the German Consul, wishing to spare the Nestorian Christians, sent word to the Vali of Mosul to return from his expedition of destruction; and when the Vali went back to Mosul there was quiet for a while again before the final storm broke. From the middle of June to the middle of July there were at least three small engagements between the Christians and the Kurds. In the absence of the Turkish regular troops the Christians were more than able to repel the aggressive Kurds and send them back their various places up to the latter part of August.

STARVING IN MOUNTAIN FASTNESS

"But very soon, the Christians had to give up their homes and take to the tops of lofty mountains. With their families and what they could bring in the way of cattle the Christians stayed in the mountains. From twelve various regions and tribes the Christians fled to mountain fastnesses and began to suffer from hunger, lack of salt and all the inconveniences of a siege, with no prospect of any immediate relief. Barley went up to fifteen dollars a load, wheat twenty dollars, salt to two dollars a pound and it could not be found anywhere. They formed a very huge camp on the top of the Tal Mountains, spreading here and there, one day's journey, with the family of Patriarch in the middle, in the famous Church of Mar Audishu, built in a rock. From it a very small spring of water comes out, which could not be sufficient to give drink to those round about. People could not eat meat without salt and could preserve nothing, and they began soon to become lean and emaciated for lack of proper food. Then food became very scarce among the masses of the people. Mr. Shlemon, who was present himself, writes: "When I went to buy some wheat from outside, people who knew me came after me crying for some bread, and we could not stop the wailing of children. Everywhere I went the mountains were luxuriant with flowers and grass. People were sitting by hundreds under mulberry trees that when the fruit was ripe they might pick up something for their little ones. Some would stay for two weeks; they had nothing to eat but herbs and berries. I saw many men who formerly were well to do and those whose 'table was always spread,' as they say; now they were dying for lack of a piece of bread and were going from house to house to get something for their little ones." Up till the middle of August that was the condition of the people. Then there was a short relief when the harvest in the mountains was ripe, but what had been sown in these regions was very little and did not last long. Sometimes the Christians would venture farther away and try to gather wheat from the fields, when often the Kurds would descend on them and kill them.

FERASHIN
SHEREFAN
MAHMEDAN

BERWARI
BARCHILAN

Hakari
SELAI
UPPER TIARI
WALTO
TAL
BAZ
JILU
LOWER TIARI
KASRAN
TKHUMA
MINIANISH
BERWAR
Chal
NARWA

THE
ASSYRIANS
OF THE
HAKARI
MOUNTAINS

"In the middle of July Mar Shimun came to Mar Audishu in Tal and called together the heads of his tribes and his Malicks (chieftains, literally kings) to consult as to what was best to do. For it was evident that soon the whole people would starve on the top of the mountains. They all felt they should go to the frontiers of Persia, a few days' journey, and ask Russian assistance to get out. The Patriarch, with forty men, risked their lives, and for two days and two nights they had nothing to eat but what they could get from the ears of the corn on the way. One whole day they had to sleep and bask before the hot sun of July and did not dare to move lest the Kurds near by should recognize them; they would be instantly killed. The Kurds saw them from a distance and took them for rocks. After much hardship they reached the Russian camp and commander in Bashkala near Salmas in Persia. No immediate assistance could be given them at that time. In the meanwhile word came from the south and west that the Pasha of Mosul was preparing a formidable army, much larger than the first one, to come and destroy the remnants of the Christians. Some of them had by this time gone back or some had still stayed in their homes with their families. The people of Tkhuma put up a great defence on September 27th and 28th. But while they were building trenches for themselves the Kurds were destroying them with guns. All they had were a few antiquated rifles and often home-made ammunition. The Turks destroyed Gundikta, Mazraya, Inner Tkhuma and many other places.

"When the people arrived at a high pass, they saw the sexton of the Church of Mar Audishu of Tal, without hat, a censer in his hand and the copy of the Gospel used in the Church service in his sack, and the censer full of incense. He was going 'to assist against the Kurds and Turks.'

For he fully believed that the presence of the Book of the Gospels would defeat the enemy.

"THE VALLEY OF DEATH"

"But the enemy had gathered from everywhere. That very same day, Saturday, September 29th, the Patriarch had arrived at Tal in time for the last rites at the funeral of his brother, Eshia (Isaiah). On the next morning some 4,000 Kurds came down upon the Patriarch and his congregation, in what seemed to be the 'the valley of death.' It was the most solemn occasion for the little band when the sound of rifles was heard from another direction toward which they were headed. 'From one party of us,' the same person present says, 'over five hundred were killed and 200 children and women were taken captive, and a very large number of sheep were carried from the people in this valley, with all the house-hold furniture that one could think of, cattle and all kind of goods which the people had saved till the present.' The Kurds had come first to the church to look for the Patriarch whom they had heard had lately arrived there. Not finding him there they unearthed the body of his dead brother, hoping to discover money or Church property. Failing in that they hurled the body down the valley, where it was afterwards seen in the water.

DEATH GRAPPLE AMONG THE CRAGS

"There were some of the Christian young men on the top of the high mountains defending Ribbat and shooting at the Kurds. When the latter heard and found out where these young men were they headed for them. These Christians were all killed, but they killed a large number of the Kurds and sold their lives dear. Then some of the Tkhuma and Tyari people headed for these high impassable mountains (Beth Dikhni and Bar Shinna). From time immemorial the Christians had planned that when they should be hard pressed by the enemy they would climb these high crags; so all who were unable to escape through the valley took refuge here. The Kurds who came from the east and from the north pressed westward and completely blocked the way of the Christians, while the Government troops and other Kurdish chiefs came from the south and isolated them. For six days and nights these men, women and children had nothing to eat. More than 2,000 were killed and over 500 were carried captive.

RUTHLESS PLUNDER OF CHRISTIAN PROPERTY

"The Turks, after losing some 300, were exhausted. As they despaired of climbing the crags, they returned and then burned the whole country of all the tribes. They destroyed more than sixty churches. From one church they carried off booty, over 180 loads, the property of the church and what the people had deposited there as being the safest place.

"It is asserted that altogether more than '300,000 sheep were carried off and not less than 50,000 head of cattle, together with all the property which these highlanders had collected for ages.' In fact, they subsisted on sheep, cattle and honey. Nearly all the beehives were either destroyed or those near their dwellings were taken by the Kurds for themselves. The destruction of the Christian property was complete - nothing was spared.

SAFE BUT PENNILESS IN A FOREIGN LAND

"These Assyrian highlanders were making for the plateaus of Salmas and Urumia in Persia, where the Russian army was. There can be nothing more pathetic, more touching and heart-rending than to leave home, church and everything behind, and then press on to another country. Their only hope for living and for subsistence was in fact that the Russian army was there. They arrived in rags, barefoot, hungry, exhausted and weary of existence; they began a life of bitter exile, exhaustion and destitution, the like of which the world has never seen. While passing near Qudshanis, the Patriarchal seat, on September 30th (N.S.) they were again attacked by wild Kurds from the mountain passes, but the young men once more showed their true mettle and betook themselves to the passes and drove them off. In the past few months some 5,000 had already escaped for their lives to the plains of Bashkala and Salmas. The Patriarch was now in at last with some 30,000 more of his people."

(By courtesy of the Board of Foreign Missions of the Presbyterian Church in the U.S.A.)

Assyrian Christian Refugees From Tyari and Tkhuma, Kurdistan, In The Autumn of 1915.
They have brought their sheep, wheat, kettles and clothes with them. They have killed one sheep and are drying the meat as a meagre provision for the future. Encamped in a popular grove, they have no shelter for the winter.

"One party had been left behind; who were besieged in the high mountain passes and had not effected an escape when the Patriarch took the 30,000 to the plains. They were about 10,000 in number and at last made their escape, most of them reaching Salmas on October 7th and 8th. Part of these remained in Bashkala and in the plain of Albak and began to gather the remnant of harvest for daily food.

Mr. Paul Shimmon of Urumia completes Mr. Shlemon's narrative thus:

SHELTERLESS ON PERSIAN PLATEAU

"The Russians for some reason or other never allowed the Assyrians who had escaped to enter the Caucasus, and so they remained in the plains of Salmas and Urumia, Persia. Winter was now approaching and various epidemics had been at work. There was hardly housing accommodation for all the refugees. The Russian authorities tried their very best to house them, but many were seen for months at large in the streets, and often washing their clothes in the bitter cold of November in the running brooks. (Salmas is about 4,500 feet above the sea level.) The Moslems would never consent to the presence of Christians in their families, as they regard them ceremonially unclean. The homes of the Salmas Christians had been already ruined during the past winter, when the Russians had left the country in the beginning of 1915, so that housing accommodations were extremely limited, and in the winter months many lived in the barns and roofless enclosures. In some houses there were twenty to thirty persons in one room.

CHRISTENDOM SENDS ASSISTENCE

"Measures of relief were at once begun by the American Missionaries, and the Russians have sent money and clothing. The Archbishop of Canterbury's Committee in London, as well as the Lord Mayor's Armenian Relief Fund, the Friends of Armenia, and other agencies, have sent most generous assistance. The contributions of the Rockefeller Foundation have been most liberal. But it is one of the saddest things in life that the majority of those who have died have perished of exposure, want, sickness and unsanitary conditions. Then at the best of all that the highlanders have been able to get in the way of relief has been a loaf of bread and one quilt for a family of five or more. The best way of appreciating what has been done is to count not those who have perished, for all would have perished, but rather those saved from the clutches of starvation and disease."

CHAPTER V

THE PLIGHT OF THE MOUNTAINEERS DURING THEIR WINTER IN AND NEAR THE PLAIN OF SALMAS

Confirmation of the above statements of conditions is given is given by the Rev. E. W. McDowell, of Salmas, who wrote on the 17th of October, 1915, as follows:

"The mass of them are without shelter of any kind and also without bedding. They are sleeping on the bare ground without covering. The rains have begun and the winter promises to set in early. What all this means to these thousands who are without shelter you need not be told.

"Since coming down a great many of them have been taken sick with a peculiar form of bowel trouble, such as the mountaineers have been having here. Dr. David Yohannan estimates there are as many as 1,000 cases. The fatality is not as great as might be expected, but there are a great many deaths. One tribe reported forty deaths within a week. I have seen the dead lying on the roadside and the women carrying their dead, orders to move on giving them little time to die decently or to be buried with respect. I gave no relief while there. Along the road they had gathered up a little grain; the Russians were giving out 1,200 loads, and help was being given on the threshing floor and from door to door. I have been making a complete list, so that when we are ready to begin we shall have them classified and shall be able to handle them. We shall give flour or wheat in weekly allowances. The cost per head will be about five shahis (2 cents). I shall refrain from giving as long as I see they can subsist on what they get from other sources.

> "Bedding is needed as badly as food. There is not much choice between dying from hunger or dying from cold."

On February 26 and on March 6, 1916, Mr. McDowell writes that he has in Salmas and environs alone 17,700 refugees under his personal supervision. They are distributed as follows: Salmas proper, 10,985, with one village yet to be heard from; Khoi, 3,200; Albak and Bashkala, 3,500. These statistics are based upon a new listing of refugees. To them have been distributed some 4,000 quilts and a little clothing. He needs more money to buy seed wheat and farm animals. He plans to assign one yoke of oxen to every four houses for their common use, and then claim the animals in the fall and trade them for grain. This plan gives the refugees the labour of the oxen during the summer and relieves them of their support next winter. As the oxen will be traded for grain after the harvest is in and grain is cheap, it should be possible to secure in this way large quantities of food for the winter months.

The following letter, written in Syriac in February, 1916, by an eyewitness, is sanctioned for publication by the Patriarch. The author is Mr. Yoel B. Rustam, of Charagushi (Urumia River), a graduate of the American College at Urumia. It was translated by Mr. Shimmon and revised by the compiler of this pamphlet. It gives a dark picture of conditions in some of the towns on the Turko-Persian border.
(See *The Near East,* July 7, 1916.):

DESPERATION IN BASHKALA

> "Those who live in Bashkala, on the frontier of Turkey and Persia, are in a most wretched condition. Up to the present (February), once only have some ninety loads of wheat been sent to them by the American missionaries. But what will this do for some 6,600 souls? Some have

gone into the fields and villages to find remnants of un-harvested wheat and pick them up to live on. Here and there a man had a sheep or a mule which he was able to take along in his flight; that has since been sold and entirely been eaten up. Now starvation is carrying them off mercilessly. Over one-third of them have died this winter. Of the 6,600, some 2,000, tired of life and existence, thought to themselves that unless we find a remedy we well starve. They said, 'Let us return to our homes in the heart of Kurdistan, where we will either find a shelter for ourselves and live, or else we will die in our homes, and be buried with our fathers.' They have gone. For the past two months not a word has ever been heard from them. Whether they are living or dead no one knows.

HOUSELESS BECAUSE NON-MOSLEM

"About 4,000 have gone to Khoi, a city in the north-western corner of Persia, and there they were in just as bad a condition. Nearly 1,500 of these have already died. There are no houses in which they can live. Khoi is now altogether inhabited by Moslems, and they could not think of polluting their premises by the presence of Christians, whom they consider religiously unclean. The Mohammedan governor compelled the Moslems, through the influence of the Russians there, to open their barns and stables for some to live in. The Christians are so lean and emaciated that death will get at them wholesale.

SHIVERING IN THE OPEN STREET

"I went into the villages of Salmas in Persia, where these Christian Highlanders are existing and went from house to house and in person saw their condition. I visited Khusrabad first, a great centre, where in normal times some 500 Syrian families used to live, beside the newly arrived

13,000 that had been scattered through the villages of this plain (Salmas). In Khusrabad there were 3,200 refugees at the beginning. For some of them there are houses in which they have been accommodated. Others are living in barns, woodsheds or stables. For others not even these are to be had, and they are living out in the streets, sitting under the walls on the highways. They suffer from cold, as they have nothing in the way of bedding and winter clothing, and winter months are severe. (It is 4,000 to 5,000 feet above sea level.) In every room, stable or barn there are living anywhere from five to thirty souls. They are given six rubles per month for their support. The ruble has very much depreciated in value, and they do not know what is best to do with this money; whether to spend it for wheat, bread, fuel, clothing, kerosene, etc. Bread is now high. Many, therefore, purchase wheat and grind it with hand-mills and then boil and eat it.

A Refugee Archdeacon

"These people are dying form actual lack of nourishment and from bitter cold. Those who are so fortunate as to be in the houses gather around the oven, [which is dug in the ground, and spread a quilt on a low table placed over the oven, in which they have put a few pieces of charcoal; and then they tuck their feet inside the quilt to get warm. They call this arrangement a *kursi*.] A quilt has been given by the missionaries to each family of five or more to spread over them. They have nothing under them, and they sleep on the bare ground. Those who are sick and those who are well are all huddled together under this *kursi*.

SICK LYING ON THE BARE GROUND

"There is hardly a house in which there are no sick. In some families two or three members are sick and they do not talk, having almost no voice left, for there is nothing for them to eat excepting dry bread, and this is secured with difficulty. Those who are well, when the sun shines stand in the sun to warm themselves, while the sick ones cannot do even that and remain on the bare ground. It was most pitiable when passing through the streets and villages; I saw sick persons prostrate on the ground under the walls here and there. There is hardly a family in which deaths have not taken place. In some places parents have died and the little ones are thrown on their own resources.

BOYS BURY THEMSELVES FOR WARMTH

"In passing through a village I came to woods on the outskirts. Near it there was a barn which was partly unroofed; it had also no door. I saw two boys of fifteen and five years of age sleeping outside the barn. On going inside I saw two other boys about ten and eight years of age. They had buried themselves in the chaff. I asked them, 'Why do you do so?' They answered, 'Because there is no room for us in the village. We have nothing to cover ourselves with, so we have buried ourselves in the chaff; it is both a quilt and a mattress.'

DOGS DISPOSE OF THE DEAD

"In one family of seven, three had died and two others were so sickly that one could not expect them to get well. I went a little way into the woods near the village and saw a person who had been buried four days previous. He had been ill and had been thrown into the woods, as he had no one to look after him. After he had died one of the boys in the barn had gone and dug a place for him in the woods and had merely thrown some dirt over him. In some cases the wife or the daughter buries the family dead. Many are so lightly covered that very soon the dogs get them out.

STARVING IN SILENCE

"Out of the 3,200 refugees in this village 1,000 had already died and there were many who were very ill. In another place I saw a mother and two children, a girl and a boy, sitting under the *kursi* warming themselves. The mother was groaning faintly, but the voice of the little girl could hardly be heard, as she had nearly starved to death. The little boy was lying quietly beside his mother and made no sound. The father and two daughters had already gone to their rest. Just to think, also, that many of these people were once well-to-do and had plenty to eat and to wear, and have now been reduced to this condition, longing for a warm meal to satisfy their cravings.

"In another village, Ula, I was told many of the people from Qudshanis (the seat of Mar Shimun, the Assyrian Patriarch) and other people were living there. At the beginning, in the fall, when they came here there were about 900 people there altogether. Now only some 350 are left, and they are in the condition that I have described already. Late in the evening, while passing through this same village, I saw a woman with nothing but a thin spread wrapped over her, and she was lying near the wall in the street, and could not be expected to live many days.

DESTITUTE UPON THE DUNGHILLS

"In another village I saw people lying on manure piles in the open and in the streets; nearly all were sick. One woman was knitting, but she was wailing bitterly and shedding floods of tears, as she thought of her former home, and now she was left at the door of strangers with nothing on which to live.

THE TERRIBLE TOLL

"From all the investigation that I was able to make and from my own personal observation, I am sure that over 5,000 out the 13,000 that had come to the plain of Salmas must have perished, and this is the opinion of others also. These refugees are too far removed from the centres of interest and are still surrounded by Moslems, so that very little practical help comes to them other than that which is given by the charitable organizations; and this is not sufficient to satisfy their hunger for bread and to give them enough clothing and bedding to be comfortable at night."

Reserving the estimated death rate for later discussion (Chap. VII.), we note that the general impression made by Mr. Rustam's narrative, and particularly his statements as regards distress in Bashkala, are confirmed by the subjoined letter from the Patriarch himself.

CHAPTER VI

LETTERS FROM THE ASSYRIAN PATRIARCH AND HIS SISTER

Mar Shimun thanks a society in London which had sent him five hundred pounds for immediate use. The letter, written on the 25th of April, 1916, is addressed to Mr. Paul Shimmon, who has translated it literally.

Mar Shimun in his Vestments

"From the Patriarchal Cell, receive prayers and blessings!
"To our beloved son Mr. Paulus³ – peace and blessings in the Lord Christ."

---

³ Editor's note: It should be highlighted that this Paul Shimmon is not Mar Paulus Shimun, the brother of the Patriarch who succeeded him as the Patriarch of the Church of the East. This Paul Shimmon was a representative of

"It is necessary that we should have written you long before this, but we thought that it would be better that we delay till we could send you the list of the names to whom money was distributed. Now we are sending the list. When it reaches your hands translate it into English and send it to the society [in London]. We have sent our acknowledgment to the society directly... We are very much afraid concerning our letters, that they may not reach you at all. In this post at Diliman [in Salmas, N.W. Persia] they do not accept registered letters for America and England.

"Indeed, we owe great gratitude to the exalted kingdom of Russia; it has assisted our nation with money, clothing and medicine. At the time that we received the money which was sent by you, it was especially beneficial to the latest refugees (the Tyari people) in Bashkala. They were dying of starvation. We hired some mules and sent wheat, which was bought by Mr. McDowell [a missionary distributing funds of the American Committee for Armenian and Syrian Relief, and also funds from England], and we also gave money for some to come here to purchase food for themselves and their families. Though we have received help for our nation from Russia, England and America, again the needs of our people are very great and heart-breaking.

STILL SICK AND STARVING

"Even now some people are dying of starvation. Very often some come to our door when they are barely able to stand on their feet from hunger. Who can refuse those who are in such condition? Now they have also a new kind of disease; their feet are swelling and getting blue, so that they cannot move at all, and they have to be assisted

---

the Patriarch. On this, see Lamassu, N, (in print), Malfono Naum Faik: Selected Writings, (London: Firodil Institute).

in everything. There are families in Bashkala [in Turkey near the frontier] whose sick members from November till now are eating bread only. How can they live? They ask for some milk when dying; it cannot be supplied them. The condition of our nation is very wretched. Mr. McDowell is now giving seed for those who can sow but they have not enough oxen. The Russians also will give, but the things are getting delayed, and we do not know what is to become of us in the meanwhile.

"We are hoping that you will do everything in your ability that the Christians in America may assist and that part of our nation may escape misery. Surma [the Patriarch's sister] has written you before this; we do not know if you have received her letters or not. We will hope that you will write us everything.

"The Grace of our Lord Christ be with you.
"Diliman, Salmas, Persia, April 12 [O.S.], 1916."

Surma, elder sister of Mar Shimun, holds a position of unique influence in the Assyrian community. She bears witness to the bitter needs of her people, and incidentally shows how they look to their Patriarch for relief.

LETTER OF SURMA, SISTER OF THE PATRIARCH

Translation of extracts from a letter from Surma, the sister of Patriarch Mar Shimun, written from Diliman, Salmas, Persia, April 30, 1916, to a friend.

"It was arranged and planned some time ago that we should leave for Bashkala and Bradost, and that the Russians would give us oxen, and the Americans seed to sow there. But this did not materialize. For even now the oxen have not come. Mr. McDowell (the American missionary) is giving some seed and oxen for some to sow here in these regions. The Russians helped us in clothing, money and medicines. But again the needs of our nation are very great. I wish you could some time see people as they eat their bread in our house, when they mix their tears with their meals. Some, you will see, their lips are dried, and they can hardly swallow their morsels.

THROWS HIMSELF ON HOSPITALITY OF PATRIARCH

"The other day when the Patriarch was leaving the Divankhana (reception room) a Tyari man threw himself, prostrate on the ground at his feet and cried out aloud, 'O Kassi' (a filial expression for the Patriarch), 'help! I and my family are nearly dying from starvation.' His color was pale, and he seemed to be out of his mind, poor man. Mar Shimun gave him some money. A woman came to the kitchen to Romé, my sister, when her tears were running down, and said that for two days she and her family had nothing to eat. She was not able to stand much longer on her feet. We fed her and gave something also for her family. There are so many such pathetic cases! How can one refuse those who are in such a condition?

"I wish that our house was as full as when we were in Qudshanis. Mr. McDowell has truly great care for the work of relief, an he is working most faithfully with all his heart, and is full of sympathy for our nation. But as I wrote above the needs are very great."

CHAPTER VII

HOW MANY REFUGEES MUST BE CARED FOR? WHAT IS THEIR DEATH RATE?

The refugees that the American Committee has thus far aided in keeping alive are the survivors of a considerably larger Christian population. The most recent statistics giving its number and composition prior to the war are tabulated in Appendix C, to which we refer those who would study the problem in its full complexity. The practical question before the American public is, however, not "How many Assyrian Christians were there two years ago," but "How many must be kept from freezing or starving to death this winter?"

The experience of last winter gives us the most valuable data on which to forecast the impending winter:

In the months of November and December, 1915, our Persian Relief Commission assisted the following in the Urumia plain alone:

Refugees from Turkey	11,392
Refugees from Persian border districts	4,397
Destitute inhabitants of the Urumia plain	13,723
	———
	29,512

In the same months the number of refugees from Turkey helped in other districts by the Commission was approximately[4] as follows:

---

[4] Later and more exact figures for Salmas, Khoi, Albak and Bashkala are given above (p.33). They cannot, however, be added to the figures for the Urumia Plain, as some weeks elapsed between the two enumerations, during which time the number of refugees at Salmas was diminished both by deaths and by migrations to Urumia.

From Salmas	12,000
From Khoi	3,500
From Albak	6,000
Armenians in Salmas	9,000
	30,500

Adding the totals we reach a grand total of 60,012. Deducting the 9,000 Armenians, we find that the Commission then had on its hands no less than 51,000 of the Assyrian Christians and of the related Christian stocks. Most of those who have survived a twelve month more of hardship will be on our hands in the coming winter. America must help feed the survivors of the 60,012, and probably a multitude beside, for times have been growing steadily worse.

It is not necessary to provide food for the dead. The high death rate makes relief work easier, but it is also its most terrible indictment.

Said William James, the psychologist: "There are topics known to every man from which he shies like a frightened horse, and which to get a glimpse of is to shun."

Have Russia, England, and, above all, neutral and smugly prosperous America, ever faced the death rate among the refugees of Urumia and Salmas?

We shall arrange our data according to the three geographical groups defined above (p.9-11).

I. MOSUL AND THE VALLEY OF THE TIGRIS (TURKEY)

Mr. Shlemon gives valuable details concerning his own Berwar region. Of his 360 neighbors in Aina d'Nuni, 20 were killed and 10 women were carried off, and 120 died in villages near Urumia in the winter of 1915-16. Of the 200 inhabitants of Duri 30 were killed or carried off, and 90 died near Urumia. Most of the inhabitants of Ikri and Malakhta were massacred; the rest were carried off. The people of Bait Baluk were forcibly converted to Islam. Of the inhabitants of the four small villages, half were killed or carried off. Of the 130 souls in Dirishki only 30 were left. From Maiyi, where Mr. Shlemon used to preach, 90 have died and 50 were alive in Persia. Haiyiz was better off than the foregoing places, for only one-third perished. In Bishemayi and lad half were dead. The last six localities mentioned were spared; but the inhabitants of one of them, Chalik, fled to Urumia and 50 per cent of them perished.

If Mr. Shlemon's figures are right, the death rate among the inhabitants of certain villages who succeeded in reaching Persia was one-half to one-third.

II. THE NATIVES OF ADARBAIJAN (PERSIA)

The losses among the natives of the Urumia region were summarized by Dr. Shedd on the 21st of May, 1915, as follows:

> "The losses to the province are stupendous, heaviest on the Christians, but involving everyone. The number of Christians killed has been at least a thousand; 4,000 more have died from disease here in Urumia, and I don't know how many among the refugees to Russia." (Persian War Relief Fund Bulletin 13, Second Ed.)

On the 25th of May, 1915, just after the Russians reoccupied Urumia, Rev. Y. M. Neesan wrote from that city to Rev. F. N.

Heazell, Letchworth, England, about the horrors which he had been through;

> "People died from the following causes: (1) From fear; (2) from their bad dwelling places; (3) from cold; (4) from hunger; (5) from typhoid fever – the dead up to now from this disease, as far as we can tell, are from 800 to 1,000. Those who died from the slaughter and raiding of villages numbered 6,000. Many died in the houses of their refuge from the causes mentioned above. About 2,000 died of those who fled (to Russia), either on the road or after their arrival there."
> (Toynbee, Document 33.)

III. THE HIGHLANDERS FROM KURDISTAN, TURKEY

This group suffered more severely than did the other two. Passing over their losses in battle (see above, p.28-29) we have evidence such as the following:

A. When the mountaineers first arrived in the Plain of Salmas there was an epidemic of intestinal trouble. Rev. E. W. McDowell wrote on the 17th of October, 1915, that a single tribe had reported forty deaths in one week. (p.32)

B. The well-known war correspondent, Mr. Phillips Price, who was in Persia when the Assyrian Highlanders began to come in, promptly asked Mr. Shipley, the British consul at Tabriz, to cable the Archbishop of Canterbury for assistance. Some months later he drew up a "Memorandum about Assyrian Refugees in Persia," which was published in "Ararat" (March, 1916, p.415 f.). He says: "In October of last year I came to

Diliman on the plain of Salmas in Northwest Persia. I had been in Urumia during September and had seen the condition of the Assyrians (mostly Orthodox, Catholic and Protestant) in the low country round that Lake. The American missionaries of Urumia were doing a great deal, and on the whole the condition of the country was not so very bad. There was housing accommodation and a good deal of corn, and it seemed as if the Americans would keep the situation in hand. But in Salmas there was a very different state of affairs." Then Mr. Price tells of the arrival, at the end of September, 1915, of 25,000 Assyrian Highlanders, led by Mar Shimun, and of the desperate lack of housing, food and clothing, also of the insufficient supply of drugs and of skilled doctors to combat typhus and dysentery. He continues: "I did not observe on my return to Salmas after a journey to Van in November any real improvement in the health of the refugees. Every day 100 or more Assyrians and Armenians were dying in the villages round Diliman, and the same is going on now....The position now is as follow: When I left Diliman for Van at the end of October, I saw in the regions round Bashkala another five or six thousand Assyrians and a sprinkling of Armenians living in caves of the rocks or in the open, and feeding on raw grains of wheat which they were picking from the ruined corn fields. On my return in January most of these were in Salmas, and so I think about 30,000 Assyrian and Armenian refugees are now there; that is after deducting 15 per cent as loss from disease in the last three months."

C. In February, 1916, Mr. Yoel B. Rustam stated that over one-third of the refugees in Bashkala had died that winter, the chief cause specified being starvation; and that of the approximately 4,000 who had gone to Khoi, nearly 1,500 had already perished, and that of the 3,200 in Khusrabad (Salmas) 1,000 had already died (p.33-35). He also was told that in Ula only some 350 were left out of about 900. On the basis of his own observations and of what he heard, he thinks that "over 5,000 out of the 13,000 that had come to the plain of Salmas must have perished" (p.36)

D. Rev. R. M. Labaree, of Urumia, now in America, thinks that the death rate did not reach one-third, but that it was in any case very high.

E. Young men from Baz were interviewed in Chicago by Mr. Paul Shimmon. They had received letters from their friends and relatives in the various villages that make up that wonderful tribe. They gave the following figures:

In the village of Arwanduz, 60 houses, 175 persons had died.

In the village of Shwawutha, 80 families, 110 persons had died.

In the village of Arghab, 60 families, 150 had perished.

In the village of Besani, 35 families, 40 had died.

Of the inhabitants of the Mata Takhtaita (Lower Village), 120 families, 145 had died.

In all, from among 355 families, 620 persons had thus met their fate.

If we count six to a family, this death rate is 29.1 per cent, or almost one-third.

From the above evidence we may draw several conclusions:

1. That the death rate varies from region to region, being larger in Salmas than in Urumia.

2. That the relief work was more effective in Urumia than in remoter places like Bashkala.

3. That disease, inadequate food, clothing and shelter continued for some months to cost many lives. Therefore, estimates made in May concerning the total death rate would be higher than those made in the preceding February.

4. That thousands of lives have been lost through causes which probably could have been prevented by the prompt use of larger sums of money than were available.

5. Since great destitution continues to prevail, the lives of the remnant of the Christian population of Persia can be saved only by prompt and generous gifts.

CHAPTER VIII

HOW THE MONEY IS SPENT

The Persian War Relief Committee, prior to its consolidation with the American Committee for Armenian and Syrian Relief, sent $70,144.00 to Persia.

The sums forwarded by the American Committee for Armenian and Syrian Relief for Persia have been as follows:

Nov. 19, 1915	$ 15,000.00
Jan. 18, 1916	25,000.00
Feb. 8	10,000.00
Feb. 15	110.00
Feb. 24	10,000.00
Mar. 15	15,000.00
Apr. 13	25,000.00
June 1	15,000.00
June 30	25,000.00
July 25	15,000.00
Sept. 25	2,000.00
Total to Oct. 5, 1916	**$157,110.00**

Up to and including the fifth day of October, 1916, the total receipts of the American Committee for Armenian and Syrian Relief for all purposes have been $1,166,185.22.

Of this amount the Rockefeller Foundation contributed $330,000.00
Of this amount other sources gave $836,185.22

All the moneys have been received by Charles R. Crane, Treasurer, 70 Fifth Avenue, New York City, and usually have been forwarded to the field through the State Department at Washington. They have been disbursed by Relief Committees of which the local consular of diplomatic representatives of the United States were members.

The Assyrian Relief Fund has become a subsidiary of the American Committee of Armenian and Syrian Relief. The Treasurer, Woodbury G. Langdon, 59 East Fifty-Ninth Street, New York City, is also a member of the larger Committee. Gifts are acknowledged each week in *The Churchman* and in *The Living Church*. The total noted in *The Churchman* of October 7, 1916, was $4,820.05.

The disbursements of the Relief committee in Urumia are tabulated in detail in quarterly statements made out by Rev. Hugo A. Muller, Treasurer. The most significant statement at hand is dated May 12th, and covers the quarter ending March 31, 1916. If printed it would occupy at least four pages of this pamphlet. We compile from it the following figures:

EXPENDITURES BY THE URUMIA RELIEF COMMITTEE,
JANUARY 1 TO MARCH 31, 1916

Administration	9,242.75[5]
Food	204,033.65
Bedding	71,731.00
Tools	909.50
Seeds	28,145.00
Oxen for Ploughing	120.00
Sanitation	25.00
Rents and Housing	155.00
Interest on Money	509.25
Transfer Charges on Money	7,058.30
Cash Grants	4,099.65
Sunnee Relief Fund	490.10
Total:	**326,519.20**

The above statement shows what it has cost to carry on the work for three months when the load was at its peak. It does not include large amounts spent in paying up the deficits of previous quarters, nor does it show heavy debts incurred for seeds (46,707.45), oxen (52,250.00), and tools (9,784.00).

———————

Moneys from various sources in England and America were administered by the same local Commission, so as to eliminate overlapping and waste. The other agencies on the field were Russian, and through the cooperation of Russian consuls it has

---

[5] These sums are in Persian silver currency. The unit is the *kran*, usually worth something under ten cents; so that by moving the decimal point one place to the left one may readily guess the values in dollars.

The table of silver money is: 1 *toman* = 10 *krans* = 200 *shahis* = 10,000 *dinars*, the latter being an imaginary entity like a mill.

Silver is rising in value in Persia, and today the *kran* costs far more than ten cents. A year ago it was worth about 8¾ cents.

been possible in nearly all cases to divide the field in such a way as to secure maximum efficiency.

The expense of administration is at a minimum, as the American Presbyterian missionaries give their time.

Representing Mar Shimun, the Assyrian Patriarch, Mr. Paul Shimmon[6] desires to express the gratitude of his people to the following agencies:

To the Russians at home through their government and their societies, and in Persia, through consuls like the Hon. Basil Nikitine, of Urumia, and through their armies which, from the Grand Duke down to the private soldier who shares his soup with refugees, have shown love to their Persian fellow Christians:

To the English, who through the Archbishop of Canterbury's Committee, The Lord Mayor's Fund, The Friends of Armenia, The Bible Lands Aid Society, Miss Barclay, and many others have contributed liberally to relief:

To the Americans in Persia, Consul Gordon Paddock, of Tabriz, the seven Presbyterian missionaries and Rev. Y. M. Neesan, who constituted a local committee for relief, and the Board of Foreign Missions of the Presbyterian Church in the U.S.A., who, on receiving news of distress in Persia organised The American Committee for Armenian and Syrian Relief. Special thanks are due also to *The Churchman* and *The Living Church* for publicity, and to the clergymen who have opened their pulpits to representatives of the cause; last nor least, to the Assyrians in America, who have undertaken great sacrifices to aid their afflicted brethren.

---

[6] See footnote 3.

CHAPTER IX

THE NEED OF THE HOUR

On the plateaus of Urumia and Salmas winter is impending. Some preparations have already been made to meet the emergencies of caring for the refugees from the highlands and the destitute natives of the plains. Just how many will need assistance cannot be known accurately in advance, but the latest estimates show that the financial burden of the relief work in Persia will be double that of the past year.

> A cablegram from W. S. Vanneman, M.D., of Tabriz, received September 27, 1916, says: "Relief Committee needs for winter: Food, $160,000; Bedding, $100,000; Clothing, $25,000; Seed, $10,000; Orphanage, $10,000; total, $305,000.

The explanation of these estimates has not yet reached America, but a letter is doubtless under way. The essential facts in it will be promptly communicated to the daily and to the religious press.

Evidently the Relief Commission intends this winter to provide more covering than one quilt to a family, and better food than coarse bread for those who may contract typhoid or dysentery. It is probable that the increased estimates are influenced also by the rise of prices, but they may likewise reflect an increase in the numbers of those who will die without our aid.

APPENDIX A

BRIEF LIST OF BOOKS ON THE ASSYRIAN OR NESTORIAN CHRISTIANS*

I. CONDITIONS PRIOR TO 1914

Benson, Arthur Christopher. The Life of Edward White Benson, Sometime Archbishop of Canterbury. London, Macmillan & Co., 1989. 2 v., 36*s*.
The Assyrian Mission is treated v. ii., p. 176-196.

Fortescue, Adrian. The Lesser Eastern Churches. London, Catholic Truth Society, 1913. xv., 468 p. Illustrations. 5*s*. net.
Critical treatment by a Roman Catholic scholar. Deals with Nestorianism and the Nestorians on pp. 54-159.

Heazell, F. N., and Mrs. Margoliouth, Editors. Kurds and Christians. London, Wells Gardner, Darton & Co., 1913. ix., 239 p., 3*s*. 6*d*. [Usually in stock at the Young Churchman Co., Milwaukee.]
Publishes interesting letters from members of the Archbishop's Mission.

Hubbard, G. E. From the Gulf to Ararat. An Expedition through Mesopotamia and Kurdistan. Edinburgh and London. William Blackwood & Sons, 1916. xv., 273 p., 10s. 6*d*. net.
By the Secretary of the Commission which laid out the boundary. Excellent illustrations.

Loofs, Friedrich. Nestorius and His Place in the History of Christian Doctrine. Cambridge, at the University Press, 1914. vii., 132 p., 3*s*. 6*d*.

Maclean, A. J. and Browne, G .F. The Catholicos of the East and His People. London, 1892.

---

* In the General Convention Edition this List contains twenty-five additional titles.

Describes ecclesiastical customs.

Miller, William. Ottoman Empire, 1801-1913. (Cambridge Historical Ser.). New York, G. P. Putnam's Sons, 1913. xvi., 547 p., $2.50.
Pp. 508-528: Bibliography.
Best brief treatment in English. Deals chiefly with Turkey in Europe.

Piolet, J. B. Les Missions Catholiques francaises au xixe siecle. Paris, Armand Colin, 1901-1903. 6 v., 60 fr.
Illustrated descriptions of the French Catholic missions in Turkey and Persia are found in the first volume.

Richter, Julius. A History of Protestant Missions in the Near East. New York, Fleming H. Revell Co., 1910. 435 p., $2.50.

Sykes, P. M. A History of Persia. London, Macmillan & Co., 1915. 2 v., 50s.
A finely illustrated narrative, ending with the revolution of 1906.

Wigram, William Ainger. An Introduction to the History of the Assyrian Church 100-640 A.D. London, Society for Promoting Christian Knowledge; New York, E. S. Gorham, 1910. xviii., 318 p., $2.

Wigram, W. A., and Wigram, Edgar T. A. The Cradle of Mankind. Life in Eastern Kurdistan. Illustrated. Map. London, A. and C. Black, 1914. xii., 373p.
Deals with the work of the Archbishop's Mission.

Wilson, Samuel Graham. Persian life and customs with scenes and incidents of residence and travel in the land of the lion and the sun. New York, Fleming H. Revell Co., 1895. Illustrated. Map. 333 p., $1.50.
By a distinguished Presbyterian missionary, who was head of American relief work in the Russian Caucasus at the time of his death in June, 1916.

Wilson, Samuel Graham. Persia: Western Mission. Philadelphia, Presbyterian Board of Publication and Sabbath-school Work, 1896. Illustrated. Map. 381 p.

Yohannan, Abraham. The Death of a Nation; or, The Ever-Persecuted Nestorian or Assyrian Christians. New York, G. P. Putnam's Sons, 1916. Illustrated. Map. $1.50.
A sketch of persecutions through the centuries, with constant references to the original sources. By the well-known Syriac lexicographer.

II. CONDITIONS DURING THE PRESENT WAR

Ararat. A searchlight on Armenia. London, The Armenian United Association of London. Monthly. July, 1913-. 6*d.*

American Committee for Armenian and Syrian Relief, 70 Fifth Avenue, New York City.
Five bulletins published under divergent titles. Sent free.

Bryce, Lord, see Toynbee, A. J.

Dillon, E. J. Persia and the Allies. (In the Contemporary Review, March, 1916, p. 315-330.) Reprinted in Littell's Living Age, May 13, 1916.

[Doughty, W. E. Comp] A National Test of Brotherhood. America's opportunity to relieve suffering in Armenia, Syria, Persia, and Palestine. [New York, American Committee for Armenian and Syrian Relief, October, 1916.]

Near East, The London Weekly.

Quarterly Papers and **Annual Reports** of the Archbishop of Canterbury's Assyrian Mission. London, Church House, and Society for Promoting Christian Knowledge.

Platt, Mary Schauffler, Editor. The War Journal of a Missionary in Persia. Chicago, Woman's Presbyterian Board of Missions of the Northwest, 1915. 51 p., 5c.

Shimmon, Paul. Massacres of Syrian Christians in N. W. Persia and Kurdistan. London, Wells Gardner, Darton & Co.; Milwaukee, The Young Churchman Co., 1916. 23 p., 20c.

Toynbee, Arnold J., Editor.
In consultation with Lord Bryce, Mr. Arnold J. Toynbee of London has compiled the following book, kindly sent to us in page proof.

Documents Relating to the Treatment of Armenian and Assyrian Christians in the Ottoman Empire and Northwestern Persia, Subsequently to the Outbreak of the European War, following upon Correspondence Between Viscount Grey of Fallodon, Secretary of State for Foreign Affairs, and Viscount Bryce.

London: Printed under the authority of His Majesty's Stationery Office, by Sir Joseph Causton & Sons, Limited, 9, Eastcheap, E. C.

After the middle of November copies can be secured for a dollar each from the American Committee for Armenian and Syrian Relief, 70 Fifth Avenue, New York City. Extracts fill three pages of the second section of the *New York Times* of Sunday, October 8, 1916.

The story of the Presbyterian Mission in Persia during the war is in preparation by Miss Rachel C. Schauffler of Lakewood, New Jersey.

The standard bibliography covering the field is: Oriental Bibliography. Berlin, Reuther & Reichard. The latest volumes (xxiii-xxiv) treat publications of the years 1909-10.

APPENDIX B

TABLE OF PRINCIPAL DATES

Turkish seizure of frontier	**August, 1906**
Anglo-Russian Convention	**August 31, 1907**
Russian occupation of Tabriz, capital of Adarbaijan, N. W. Persia	**April 30, 1909**
Russian occupation of Urumia, Persia	**December, 1911**
Turkish evacuation of frontier districts	**Autumn, 1912**
Turko-Persian Frontier Commission	**1913-14**
Kurds drive Cossacks from Tergawar	**October 1, 1914**
Turko-Kurdish attack on Urumia	**October 9-12, 1914**
Turkish torpedo-boats attack Odessa	**October 29, 1914**
Russia declares war on Turkey	**November 3, 1914**
Fetwa on Holy War read, Constantinople	**November 14, 1914**
Russian defeat at Miandub, South of Urumia	**About December 25, 1914**
Turkish advance and defeat at Sarykamish (Kars region)	**December 25, 1914- January 5, 1915**
Evacuation of Urumia by the Russians	**January 2, 1915**
Evacuation of Salmas by the Russians	**January 4, 1915**
Evacuation of Tabriz by the Russians	**January 5, 1915**
Plundering and destruction of seventy-odd Urumia villages; massacres in the plain	**January 2-10, 1915**
Turkish occupation of Tabriz	**January 8-30, 1915**
Russian reoccupation of Tabriz	**About February 5, 1915**
Turkish occupation of Urumia	**January 4-May 20, 1915**
Turkish massacre of Bishop Mar Dinkha and others from the French Mission, Urumia	**February 23, 1915**
Turkish massacre of men of Gulpashan	**February 25, 1915**
Massacre at Salmas	**About March 5, 1915**
Capture of Mar Elia, the Russian Syrian Bishop; and others held for large ransoms	**March 9, 1915**
Reoccupation of Salmas by Russians	**About March 8, 1915**
Massacre of Armenians, in Van Army	**About April 1, 1915**
Arrival of Halil Bey's forces in Urumia	**April 16, 1915**
Massacre in Gawar and other districts in Turkey	**April, 1915**
Turks besiege Armenians in Van	**April 20-May 18, 1915**
Defeat and retreat of Halil Bey's army in Salmas	**May 1-10, 1915**
Reoccupation of Urumia by Russians	**May 24, 1915**
Vali of Mosul begins attack on Highlanders and	**June, 1915**

destroys Lower Tyari
Attacks continue during summer, when
Highlanders withdraw to top of mountains.

Second flight of Christians from Urumia	**August 6, 1915**
Return of the Christians to Urumia	**About August 24, 1915**
Attack and destruction of Tkhuma	**September 27-28, 1915**
Flight of Patriarch to Salmas	**September 29-October 7, 1915**
Patriarch's visit to Grand Duke Nicholas in Tiflis to obtain relief	**January, 1916**
Patriarch's first visit to Urumia	**January-February, 1916**
Petrograd announces defeat of Turks near Ushnu	**August 22, 1916**
Petrograd announces recapture of Mush	**August 24, 1916**

APPENDIX C

NEW STATISTICS OF THE ASSYRIAN CHRISTIANS AND RACIALLY RELATED GROUPS PRIOR TO THE WAR

In the following estimates we are concerned with six groups, mostly of ancient origin. Some of the old names, like "Syrian" and "Chaldean," are claimed by more than one of them, and are therefore ambiguous.

1. The Assyrian Christians, often called Syrians or Nestorians (p. 7). Their patriarch is Mar Shimun (p. 11).
2. The Jacobites, reorganized by Jacob Baradai in the second half of the sixth century.
3. Those Roman Catholic Uniats, living in the Dominican mission of Mosul in the archdiocese of Bagdad, whose ancestors were Nestorians. They are spoken of in Mosul as "Chaldeans," though in Persia that term is more loosely used.
4. The Uniats, whose ancestors were Jacobites, are known in the Mosul region as "Syrian Catholics," though elsewhere, as in Persia, the term does not seem to have that restricted meaning.
5. Converts to the Russian Church (p. 11), designated as Syrian Orthodox.
6. Protestants, principally connected with the American Presbyterians (p. 8). In or near Urumia, however, the Baptists, Plymouth Brethren, American Lutherans, and the German Orient Mission have, or at least have had, institutions of some sort.[§]

[§] Sources of some of the above statements: - (a) Jacobites, Chaldeans and Syrian Catholics: A. Fortescue in *Catholic Encyclopedia*, v., New York, 1909, 236; G. Oussani, *ibid.*, xi., 724; Rödiger and Nestle in Herzog-Hauck, *Realencyklopädie*, 3. Aufl., viii., Leipzig, 1900, 570; (b) Protestants: see W. A. Shedd in the *New Schaff-Herzog Encyclopedia of Religious Knowledge*, vol. viii., New York, 1910, 472; (c) for modern Syria, including the five governmental

The figures tabulated below are not based on actual count, but are estimates from native sources. The data for the Tigris region were furnished to Mr. Paul Shimmon on June 13, 1916, by the Rev. Abraham Shlemon, of Aina d'Nuni in the region of Berwar near Mosul. The statements for the Urumia and Salmas regions come from Mr. Shimmon, whose home is in the city of Urumia. The statistics of the Highlanders of Kurdistan were given to Mr. Shimmon in August, 1915, by His Beatitude Mar Shimun, the Patriarch of the Assyrian Christians, by Bishop Mar Yaw Alaha, of Duri, in the region of Berwar, and by the chieftain Malick Khoshaba.

I. MOSUL AND THE VALLEY OF THE TIGRIS (BY FAMILIES).*

		Nestorian	Jacobite[t]	Roman Catholic	Protestant	Mixed[‡]
Mosul	8,700		1,900	6,800		
Sapna	875	105		740	30	
Zibar	1,457	62		595		800
Bohtan	460	50		60	100	250
Berwar	450	450				

---

divisions of Aleppo, Beyrout, the Lebanon, Damascus and Jersualem, see Jessup and Hoskins, *ibid.*, xi., 1911, 232. On the dialects see the introduction to A. Yohannan, *A Modern Syriac-English Dictionary,* Part I., New York, 1900.

* Lack of space forbids printing here the detailed estimates, village by village. The compiler has communicated them to the American Geographical Society for inclusion among the notes in *The Geographical Review.*

[t] The Jacobites of the regions of Mardin and Diarbekir are not included. According to S. Vailhé in the Catholic Encyclopedia, Vol. X., 1911, p. 599, the Mission of Mosul "includes the southeast of Mesopotamia, Kurdistan, and the northeast of Armenia Major, a stretch of territory covering the vilayets of Mosul, Bitlis, Van and a part of Diarbekir. Besides the Arabs, Kurds and Mussalman Turks (about 3,000,000), and the Yezidis or devil-worshippers (about 30,000), the Mission numbers 300,000 schismatic Armenians; 70,000 Jacobites; 30,000 Nestorians; 5,000 Protestants and 10,000 Jews. The Catholics of all the rites scattered through the territory amount to 80,000."

[‡] Cases in which the figures for the Christian families in a village cannot be classified under any single rubric. It is probable that more than half of the mixed groups consist of Roman Catholics.

| Total families. | 11,942 | 667 | 1,900 | 8,195 | 130 | 1,050 |
| " individuals. at six to a family. | 71,652 | 4,002 | 11,400 | 49,170 | 780 | 6,300 |

II. ADARBAIJAN (PERSIA)

Urumia is divided into three parts called rivers (Turkish *chai*). The three rivers empty into the west side of the Lake of Urumia, and together include about seventy villages. In the following list the "rivers" are numbered 1 to 3.

1. Nazlu Chai; 2. Urumia Chai; 3. Baranduz Chai; 4. Sulduz, south of Lake Urumia; 5. Mergawar, on the frontier southwest of Urumia; small villages subject to the Kurds; 6. Tergawar, on the frontier north of Mergawar; includes the large village of Mawana, Qurana, etc.; 7. The Anzal district, north of Urumia, and politically part of it, includes the village of Gavilan, etc.; 8. Bradost (Baradost) is a valley northwest of Urumia, containing one or two Christian villages. 9. The district of Salmas, in normal times inhabited chiefly by Mohammedans. The chief town is Diliman. Khusrabad (Khosrowa), Ula, etc., are large villages. The former is a centre of Roman missions. 10. Sennah, in Persian Kurdistan, has a few families.

Before the war these ten groups in Persia were commonly estimated at about 7,000 families. At five to a family we reach the estimate of population given by the Rev. Dr. Shedd, of Urumia, namely, 35,000. Rev. Mr. Labaree writes that in his opinion the outside number for the *Assyrians* in the Urumia region is 30,000. This is, of course, exclusive of Armenians.

The denominational groupings are variously stated: cf. Catholic Encyclopedia xi, 724, cf. viii, 193; and New Schaff-Herzog Encyclopedia viii, 473. For its Western Persia Mission the Board of Foreign Missions of the Presbyterian Church in the United States of America reports in 1916 the figures of the previous year: communicants, 2,804; adherents, 3,172. (Seventy-ninth Annual Report, 1916, p. 126-127.)

III. THE HIGHLANDERS OF KURDISTAN, TURKEY (BY FAMILIES).

Most of them are Ashiret, or tribal (semi-independent); the rest are Rayat, or subject. Almost all are Nestorians.

Tyari	5,000
Tkhuma	2,500
Baz	800
Tal	700
Diz	600
Jilu	2,500
Berwar (Qudshanis included)	900
Lewan (West of Julamerk)	300
Serai (45 miles east of Van)	300
Eleven villages around Serai	400
Norduz (on Van-Julamerk road)	200
Albak (near Bashkala)	300
Gawar	400
Six villages in Nerwan and Rekan	200
Shemsdinan and Mar Bishu, estimated	200
Total families	15,300
Total individuals at six to a family	91,800

These round numbers leave considerable room for discussion.

SUMMARY OF THE FOREGOING FIGURES.

In converting the estimates of families into estimates of individuals it is safe to multiple by five in the Urumia region and by six in the Highland districts, as also in the region of Mosul and the valley of the Tigris, if we may generalize the testimony of Mr. Shlemon of Berwar. Our tabulations are therefore based on six for Groups I. and III., and on five for Group II.

	Families	Persons
I. Mosul and the Valley of the Tigris	11,942	71,652
II. Adarbaijan (Persia)	7,000	35,000
III. The Highlanders of Kurdistan, Turkey	15,300	91,800
Estimated total of Assyrian Christians, including some of Racially Related Groups	34,242	198,452

If we take the above statistics at their face value we reach as maximum estimates of the numbers of individual Assyrian Christians who recognize Mar Shimun as their patriarch, the following:

I. Mosul and the Valley of the Tigris	4,002
II. Adarbaijan (Persia), about	35,000
III. The Highlanders of Kurdistan, Turkey	91,800
	130,800

From this total there must be subtracted those who have become Syrian Orthodox, about	15,000
Maximum estimate for those recognizing Mar Shimun as their patriarch, prior to the war	**115,800**

Let us test this result. Says Adrian Fortescue, whom no one will accuse of partiality to the Nestorians: "The largest number I find is given by Silbernagl, 150,000; the smallest 70,000. Cuinet, who is generally sound, gives 100,000." (*The Lesser Eastern Churches*, 1913, p. 128.) As the estimate of 70,000 was given by Smith and Dwight in 1833, and that by Cuinet published in 1892, the above maximum estimates for 1914-15 are probably not so very much too large.

These estimates, it should be remembered, are for conditions prior to the war. To fit the present day they must be reduced by making allowances for the shocking death rate (see above p. 41-43).

THE ARCHBISHOP OF CANTERBURY

has sent the letter, printed below, to Mr. Paul Shimmon, personal representative of the Assyrian Patriarch. Rt. Rev. Daniel S. Tuttle, D.D., Presiding Bishop, has added his endorsement in a letter to Mr. Shimmon, dated September 27, 1916.

Lambeth Palace, S. E. (London),
9th August, 1916

Dear Mr. Shimmon,

I have now received your interesting letter of July 13th, and I rejoice to hear of the friendly welcome which you have received in the United States and of the response which is made to your appeal on behalf of both Assyrians and Armenians. The published letter signed by sixteen American Bishops is a very weighty document.* It is hardly necessary that I should add to what I have already written to you and on your behalf, but I cordially approve of your stating, as opportunity offers, that you have my full approval in the endeavor you are making, and that with all my heart I wish God-speed to your efforts. The distresses of your people are appalling. No gifts of money, however generous, can really assuage their sorrows, but we can at least show them that their fellow-Christians in other parts of the world are mindful of the terrors, the sorrows, and the strain which they have been called upon to undergo. Pray let me hear again from you before long.

I remain, with every good wish,
Yours very truly,
(Signed) RANDALL CANTUAR.

The Archbishop also sent a letter to Bishop Tuttle, dated September 14, 1916, from which we quote, by permission:

---

* Printed in the first or General Convention edition, and on special folders.

"Sad record which reaches us seems to enhance the gravity of the situation. I do not think it is possible to exaggerate the distress of the Christian men, women and children now prevailing everywhere in the wide area on the borderland of Turkey and Persia wherein, for so many generations, the Christian population has held to its faith in face of unending oppression, cruelty and misrule. Anything which can at the present time be done to augment the relief which we are trying to render to them will be most welcome."

The Right Reverend Daniel S. Tuttle, D. D., Presiding Bishop of the Protestant Episcopal Church in the United States of America has authorized the publication of the following original prayer, which we copy from his autograph letter of the 3d of October, 1916.

A PRAYER FOR THOSE IN DISTRESS

O God, our Heavenly Father, who art unceasing in goodness and loving kindness to the sons of men, and of pitying mercy towards them that suffer, we commend to Thy Almighty care and protection the afflicted peoples of the distant East, the Assyrians and Armenians and the Syrians living in Turkey and in the Russian Caucasus, in Persia and in Egypt. Relieve we pray Thee, the distress and torture of the Christians in those border lands. Assuage their grief. Supply their wants. Save them from massacre, destitution, famine and from the horrors of deportation; and the women and innocent children from the shameful perils of captivity. Incline the hearts of all the world to assist them to rebuild their ruined homes and to secure seed to sow and clothes to wear. May the good example of those who have kept the faith and died the martyrs' death avail to strengthen them that remain to resist temptation and to stand the firmer for righteousness and truth. And, by Thy grace, may dutiful submission to Thy will abide with them, and a sweet spirit of resignation, and even of forgiveness, and may the days of their suffering be shortened, to Thine honor and glory, through the merits and mercies of Jesus Christ our Saviour. Amen.

PRACTICAL HINTS

For free copies of this pamphlet, and for folders suitable for distribution in churches, send to the American Committee for Armenian and Syrian Relief, 70 Fifth Avenue, New York, or to *The Churchman,* 381 Fourth Avenue, New York, or to *The Living Church,* Milwaukee, Wis. Please specify the edition wanted (see p. 56).

Copies of the General Convention edition may be obtained in England through Rev. F. N. Heazell, The Reactory, Letchworth.

Beware of solicitors, even though equipped with apparently genuine credentials from Oriental prelates.

The expenses of the Committee are met by special subscriptions, so that every dollar you give will be sent to the sufferers.

Relief work among the Assyrian Christians and related groups in Northwestern Persia this winter will demand $305,000.00 (see page 47).

Checks may be drawn to the order of "Charles R. Crane, Treasurer," and sent to the American Committee for Armenian and Syrian Relief, 70 Fifth Avenue, New York. They may be specially marked "For Assyrian Relief."

"Lord, when saw me Thee an hungered and fed Thee?"